*The Conquest*
*of American Inflation*

# The Conquest
# of American Inflation

Thomas J. Sargent

PRINCETON UNIVERSITY PRESS

PRINCETON AND OXFORD

Second printing, and first paperback printing, 2002
Paperback ISBN 0-691-09012-2

*The Library of Congress has cataloged the cloth edition of this book as follows*

Sargent, Thomas J.
The conquest of American inflation / Thomas J. Sargent.
p.  cm.
Includes bibliographical references and index.
ISBN 0-691-00414-5 (alk. paper)
1. Inflation (Finance)—United States.   I. Title.
HG540.S27  1999
332.4'1'0973—dc21      98-38410

British Library Cataloging-in-Publication Data is available

The publisher would like to acknowledge the author of this volume for
providing the camera-ready copy from which this book was printed

Printed on acid-free paper. ∞

www.pup.princeton.edu

Printed in the United States of America

10   9   8   7   6   5   4   3

ISBN-13: 978-0-691-09012-2 (pbk.)

*To Carolyn*

# Contents

# *Preface*

This essay is about how policy makers in the United States after World War II learned to believe and act upon a version of the natural unemployment rate hypothesis, either a rational expectations version characterized by a cross-equation restriction or an adaptive expectations version characterized by a restriction on a sum of weights in a distributed lag. Within a rational expectations version, Kydland and Prescott identified a credibility problem that makes knowing the natural rate hypothesis insufficient to cause a government to set inflation as low as it should. Kydland and Prescott predicted worse outcomes than Phelps had found in 1967 under adaptive expectations. Using Phelps's work as an ingredient, this essay continues an effort started by Christopher Sims to create an econometric model of an adaptive economic policy that can produce outcomes persistently better than the time-consistent one predicted by Kydland and Prescott. I use a model within which the government learns to act on an approximate but good enough version of the natural rate hypothesis.

This is the text of my Marshall lectures at the University of Cambridge in October 1996 and my Nemmers inaugural lecture at Northwestern University in May 1997. I also gave lectures at the University of Michigan, the University of Pennsylvania, the University of Chicago, Yale University, the University of Tel Aviv, the Bank of Israel, the Federal Reserve Banks of San Francisco and Chicago, and the Board of Governors of the Federal Reserve System. I thank those places for inviting me.

For encouragement and helpful comments and suggestions, I thank Andrew Abel, Martin Eichenbaum, François Velde, Kenneth Kasa, David Kreps, Carolyn Sargent, Jose Scheinkman,

Robert Solow, Christopher A. Sims, Nancy Stokey, Bharat Trahan, and especially Marco Bassetto, In-Koo Cho, Aaron Tornell, George Evans, Timothy Cogley, Lars Hansen, and Ramon Marimon. I thank Nathan Grawe, Mark Wright and Chao Wei for extraordinarily intelligent research assistance. The research behind this essay was supported by grants from the National Science Foundation to the National Bureau of Economic Research.

*The Conquest*
*of American Inflation*

# 1
## The Rise and Fall of U.S. Inflation

### Facts

Figure 1.1 plots the annual rate of inflation in the U.S. consumer price index since World War II. Inflation was low during the late 1950's and early 1960's, swept upward into the 1970's, and then fell abruptly with Volcker's stabilization in the early 1980's. If we take for granted that inflation is under the control of the Federal Reserve, how can we explain these observations?

### Two interpretations

This essay evaluates two interpretations based on policy makers' beliefs about the Phillips curve. In both, the Federal Reserve authorities learn the natural rate of unemployment theory from a combination of experience and *a priori* reasoning. The stories differ in how the natural-rate theory is cast. I call the first story the triumph of natural-rate theory and the second one the vindication of econometric policy evaluation.[1,2]

---

[1] Our subtext is Keynes's observation that 'madmen in authority are the slaves of some defunct economist.'

[2] I recommend J. Bradford De Long's (1997) informative and colorful description of the emergence of high inflation in the U.S. in the 1970's. De Long uses elements of both stories. De Long's discussant John Taylor (1997) endorses a version of the first story and asserts his view that '... changing economic theories and opinions about inflation are the ultimate cause of the changes in actual inflation.'

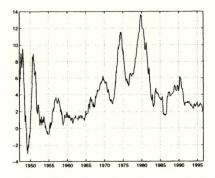

**Figure 1.1.** Monthly inflation, CPI,
all items. 13-month centered moving
average.

*The triumph of natural-rate theory*

Adherence to the gold standard and then to the rules of Bretton Woods gave the U.S. low inflation and low expectations of inflation. In 1960, Paul Samuelson and Robert Solow found a Phillips curve in the U.S. time series for inflation and unemployment. They taught that the Phillips curve was exploitable and urged raising inflation to reduce unemployment.[3] Within a

---

[3] This account comes from reading page 192 of Samuelson and Solow (1960). Important qualifications appear elsewhere in their paper. On page 193 they express reservations about exploiting the trade-off when they say that 'it would be wrong, though, to think that our Figure 2 menu that relates obtainable price and unemployment behavior will maintain its same shape in the longer run. What we do in a policy way during the next few years might cause it to shift in a definite way. ... it might be that the low-pressure demand would so act upon wage and other expectations as to shift the curve downward in the longer run – so that over a decade, the economy might enjoy higher price stability than our present-day estimate would indicate.' My two stories omit many details, including important reservations in Samuelson and Solow (1960) and the research inspired by it. (Jorge Luis Borges's character Funes the Memorious did the opposite by remembering so much that he would see no pattern or model.) But please read Chapter 10 before thinking that I treat Samuelson and Solow unkindly.

decade, Samuelson and Solow's recommendation was endorsed by many macroeconomists and implemented by policy makers. To everyone's dismay, over time the Phillips curve shifted adversely: inflation rose, but unemployment on average didn't fall. In the meantime, Edmund Phelps (1967), Milton Friedman (1968), and Robert E. Lucas, Jr. (1972) created and refined the concept of the natural rate of unemployment which assigned a central role to people's expectations about inflation in locating the Phillips curve. The natural-rate theory allowed only a temporary trade-off between inflation and unemployment and explained the observed adverse shifts in the Phillips curve. Its rational expectations version meant that policy makers should ignore any temporary Phillips curve trade-off and strive only for low inflation. These ideas diffused among academics, then influenced policy makers, and ultimately promoted the lower inflation rates of the 1980's and 1990's. Thus, events were shaped by policy makers' beliefs - some false, others true - and the actions those beliefs inspired.

Robert E. Lucas, Jr. (1976) used Samuelson and Solow's method for deducing policy recommendations from a statistical Phillips curve as an example of erroneous methodology. While Lucas's reasoning soon banished Samuelson and Solow's method from scientific research centers in economics, the method survived and prospered within the Federal Reserve System, a fact that inspires an alternative account of post 1960 inflation in the U.S.

*The vindication of econometric policy evaluation*

The alternative interpretation ascribes Volcker's conquest of inflation partly to the success of the econometric and policy-making procedures that Lucas challenged in his Critique. The vindication story begins with the same initial conditions, namely, the history of inflation and unemployment and the associated state of expectations inherited by policy makers in 1960.[4] Similarly, this story assumes that the data conformed to the natural rate hypothesis, whether or not the policy makers realized it. Policy makers accepted Samuelson-Solow's 1960 Phillips curve as an exploitable trade-off; they also adopted their methods for learning from data and for deducing policy recommendations. Recurrently, they re-estimated a distributed lag Phillips curve and used it to reset a target inflation-unemployment rate pair. Phelps, Friedman, and Lucas advocated identifying peoples' expectations of inflation as the hidden state variable positioning the Phillips curve, but they were ignored. Decisions emerged from econometric policy evaluation. That method revealed an adversely shifting Phillips curve, which when interpreted mechanically,[5] led policy makers to pursue lower inflation.[6]

To complete the vindication story, I describe the post 1960 history of U.S. inflation in terms of an adaptive theory of policy. The theory originates with a minimal departure from rational expectations[7] and accounts for features of the data that rational expectations misses. Compelling arguments made in the 1970's by proponents of rational expectations changed the way macroeconomists built and estimated models, and left adaptive expectations outmoded. Nevertheless, I recall adaptive expectations. The original form of adaptive expectations posited that agents form expectations about a variable $x$ as a fixed geometric distributed lag of past values of $x$ (Cagan (1956), Friedman (1957), Muth (1960)). A more modern form incorporates forecasting functions like those in rational expectations models but with coefficients that adapt to fit recent data. In both forms,

---

[4] The vindication story has been told before, for example, by Sims (1988) and Chung (1990).

[5] I.e., without trying to identify expectations in a natural-rate Phillips curve.

[6] Or would have led. See Chapter 9.

[7] It incorporates more optimizing behavior than do the three examples in Lucas (1976) or the one in Lucas (1972), each of which assumed arbitrary government policy.

adaptive expectations play essential roles in generating the inflation observations and in improving theoretical outcomes. To construct the historical account, I first revisit old issues such as whether, in a distributed lag model for expectations of inflation, the sum of the weights on lagged inflation should be unity, as proposed by Solow (1968) and Tobin (1968). I explain the significance of this issue within the context of Phelps' (1967) model of setting inflation under the natural-rate hypothesis. I then connect a sequence of ideas: drifting coefficients, self-confirming equilibria, least squares and other adaptive or recursive learning algorithms, convergence of least squares learners to self-confirming equilibria, and recurrent dynamics along escape routes from self-confirming equilibria. I integrate these ingredients to account for the post-War II inflation in terms of drifting coefficients that embody the evolving beliefs of an adaptive government adjusting its naive view of a Phillips curve in the light of recent evidence. I take an important idea from Sims (1988): an adaptive model allows a government to learn from past attempts to exploit the Phillips curve and to discover a version of the natural-rate hypothesis that instructs it to reduce inflation. I add to Sims's insight an account of how the escape route dynamics of our adaptive system can spontaneously generate regime shifts caused by their learning-inspired nonlinearities.

This account of the post 1960 inflation process denies that inflation policy is made in a vacuum or occurs as a natural experiment, as in Lucas (1972 or 1976). Instead, it asserts that inflation policy emerges gradually from an adaptive process.[8] Though this vindication story backs away slightly from rational expectations, it imposes more restrictions on government policy than does the triumph of the natural-rate story, which occasionally shifts free parameters describing government behavior to

---

[8] See Sims (1982) and Sargent (1983) for discussions of whether regime changes ought to be posited in explaining macroeconomic time series.

fit the facts. Also, the retreat from rational expectations is sufficiently small that the cross-equation restrictions forming the econometric hall mark of rational expectations continue to play a leading role.

## Readers's guide

Because I assemble diverse arguments, some of which appear at first to be detours, I offer the following guide. The reader who temporarily loses the path of the argument can reorient himself by consulting this guide. A glossary defines key terms.

### The Lucas critique

Chapter 2 reviews and modifies the Lucas Critique. It describes circumstances in which the Critique is ignored, recalls Sims's (1982) doubts, and sets the stage for the adaptive models in the second half of the essay.

### Time-consistency and credible plans

Chapters 3 and 4 describe rational expectations models and the literature on sustainable plans in macroeconomics. Chapter 4 is technically difficult, but can be skipped without losing the book's main line argument. Chapter 3 describes a one-period version of the Kydland-Prescott economy and Chapter 4 studies an infinite horizon version. When supplemented with best response or least squares dynamics, the model of Chapter 3 explains the acceleration of inflation but not the stabilization under Volcker. Because it explains more, Chapter 4's model of a repeated economy with credible government policies predicts less. Multiple equilibria are essential to the theory of credible plans and present enough outcomes paths to subvert confidence that we can explain either the acceleration in inflation or Volcker's stabilization with this model.

The agnosticism from Chapter 4 is familiar to students of game theory (see e.g., Maskin and Tirole (1994)). The remainder of the essay explores alternative modifications of the basic model that might produce the observed outcome history. Relative to the sustainable-plan setting of Chapter 4, I shall introduce two restrictions on the government: one on its strategy space, another on its knowledge. I adhere to the rational expectations benchmark and economize on free parameters. I embrace minimalism to discipline my venture into the wilderness of bounded rationality.

*Adaptive expectations and the Phelps problem*

Chapter 5 starts our departure from rational expectations by returning to the origin of the natural-rate hypothesis with Phelps (1967). This chapter considers two ideas: the Phelps problem and the induction hypothesis. The Phelps problem uses an empirical Phillips curve to compute an optimal government decision rule for setting inflation. The induction hypothesis, embedded both in the Friedman-Cagan adaptive expectations model and in the Solow-Tobin test of the natural-rate hypothesis, restricts the sum of weights on lagged inflation in an expectations-formation equation. The authors of that restriction misinterpreted it as a long-run implication of rationality. (Lucas (1972) and Sargent (1971) showed that rational expectations instead imposes a cross-equation restriction.) But when the empirical Phillips curve fulfills the induction hypothesis, the Phelps problem recommends lower inflation rates than when it doesn't. The basis of the Phelps problem, the empirical Phillips curve, is arbitrary throughout Chapter 5. The remaining chapters strive to identify this curve and to explain the Volcker stabilization.

*Equilibrium under misspecification*

Chapter 6 detours to introduce a new equilibrium concept within the simplest context. I call it an equilibrium with an optimal misspecified forecasting function, and use it to modify a famous model of Margaret Bray (1982). The equilibrium concept merges ideas of Halbert White (1982) with those of John Muth (1961). It mutually determines both a true model and an approximating model. This chapter sets forth a mechanism by which subtly mistaken beliefs can substantially influence outcomes. I apply this equilibrium concept to the Phillips curve example, and use the results to interpret the simulations in Chapter 8.

*Two types of self-confirming equilibria*

Chapter 7 returns to an unresolved issue from Chapter 5, the arbitrary empirical Phillips curve used in the Phelps problem. Chapter 7 introduces the concept of self-confirming equilibrium to restrict the empirical Phillips curve. I use the concept of a self-confirming equilibrium to interpret and extend King and Watson's (1994) empirical work on the U.S. Phillips curve. Within a vector autoregression, King and Watson described alternative resolutions of the simultaneous equation problem (i.e., should you estimate the Phillips curve by regressing inflation on unemployment or unemployment on inflation?) and their implications for impulse responses to various shocks. By ascribing different prior beliefs to the government, different directions of fit affect self-confirming equilibria. I describe the equilibrium consequences of the direction of fit partly in response to the recent literature proclaiming that the Phillips curve is alive and well.[9] The papers that detect the most validity for the Phillips curve put inflation on the left side.

Chapter 7 displays two examples of self-confirming Phillips curves, designed to match King and Watson's classical and Keynesian identifying assumptions. In each example, beliefs are verified by large data samples. As a means of sustaining better than Nash (Kydland-Prescott time consistent) outcomes, self-confirming equilibria are disappointing. They cause the empirical Phillips curve to deny the induction hypothesis and make the solution of the Phelps problem reproduce the Nash equilibrium

---

[9] See Jeffrey Fuhrer (1995).

outcome, or something worse. This outcome pattern reflects how the self-confirming equilibria are equivalent or close to the Nash equilibria found in Chapter 3.[10] But Chapter 7 closes with a promising result. It displays an equilibrium where the private sector's forecasting model is wrong in a subtle way and where the outcome is substantially better than the Nash outcome.

## Adaptive expectations

There is neither learning nor inference in the models of Chapter 7, only self-confirming sets of government beliefs and policies. Chapter 8 explores additional outcomes when learning is added by slightly modifying the models. I add at most one new free parameter to the models of Chapter 7.[11] I simply replace the assumption that the government and private agents know the moments used to compute the Phillips curve and forecasting function with the assumption that they must estimate sample moments. This leads to Kreps's anticipated utility model, a 1990's adaptive expectations model. I describe two versions of this model that differ in a single gain parameter that sets a data forgetting rate.

If we use a gain that eventually implements least squares and weights all past observations equally, then convergence theorems imply that self-referential systems with least squares learning eventually converge to self-confirming equilibria. Consequently, with such a gain sequence, the adaptive system ultimately adds no outcomes to the pessimistic analysis of Chapter 7. However, new outcomes occur under a gain parameter that is constant and discounts past data. This algorithm is sensible where the government and private agents suspect coefficient drift. The government's use of such an algorithm arrests the force pushing the system toward a self-confirming equilibrium

---

[10] Such an outcome is familiar from the literature about learning schemes that converge to Nash equilibria.

[11] It depends on whether we count alteration of the gain sequence from $\frac{c}{i^\alpha}$ with $\alpha = 1$ to one with $\alpha = 0$ as adding a free parameter or just changing the setting of a parameter $\alpha$ present but hidden in the rational expectations model.

and fosters recurrent deviations away from a self-confirming equilibrium.

Striking simulations under the constant-gain algorithm exhibit spontaneous stabilizations resembling the advent of Volcker. But there is no Volcker. The constant-gain algorithm learns the natural-rate hypothesis in exactly the form that Solow and Tobin expressed it. That and the Phelps problem produce the stabilization. Drifting coefficients play a key role in these stabilizations. I interpret coefficient drift and the behavior that it implies in terms of the categories of Chapters 5, 6, and 7: the induction hypothesis and its impact on the outcome of the Phelps problem; and the ability of a misspecified model that uses the induction hypothesis to approximate the truth. The simulations exhibit an interplay between mean dynamics that push the system toward a pessimistic, self-confirming outcome, and random activity along an escape route from self-confirmation that recurrently expels the system toward the Ramsey outcome. [12] The escape-route dynamics make the drift in the random coefficients seem purposeful. The stabilizations in the simulations originate in monetary policy rules that embody the government's shifting model of the Phillips curve and reflect activation of the induction hypothesis within the Phelps problem. Properties of these simulations form the basis for our vindication of econometric policy evaluation, which we pursue econometrically in Chapter 9.

---

[12] Our work bears a close connection to that of Evans and Honkapohja (1993) and some of the literature they cite. Evans and Honkapohja describe how agents' use of a drifting coefficient model can induce recurrent shifts between two locally stable rational expectations equilibria. They use this as a way to generate endogenous regime shifts. The mechanism we describe has many common components with theirs but differs in that our system recurrently escapes to something that is not an equilibrium.

*Empirical vindication*

Chapter 9 computes econometric estimates for two of our 1990's adaptive models for U.S. data and uses them to confirm the vindication story. They reveal how the adaptive algorithm would have approximated the induction hypothesis soon enough to send timely advice through the Phelps problem. The econometric estimates present the mystery of why the stabilization was postponed.

Chapter 10 assembles the various components of our arguments and discusses how they bear on a research program that contemplates occasional and disciplined backing away from rational expectations.

## *Raw and filtered Data*

Despite its disrepute within important academic and policy-making circles,[13] the Phillips curve persists in U.S. data. Simple econometric procedures detect it.

Figure 1.2 plots the unemployment rate for white men over 20 years of age against the CPI inflation rate. Many students of the Phillips curve advocate adjusting the aggregate unemployment rate for movements in the demographic mix. Using an unemployment rate for the single group, white males over 20, helps coax a Phillips curve from the data. Filtering out slowly moving components allows the eye to spot an inverse relationship between inflation and unemployment at business-cycle frequencies. Figure 1.3 plots business cycle components of inflation and unemployment. A frequency decomposition

---

[13] We witnessed the battering from the press, and the silence from his fellow Governors, that greeted Federal Reserve Board Vice Chairman Alan Blinder's comments in July 1994 at Jackson Hole. I do not believe that Blinder's comments would have excited controversy or exception at any leading macroeconomics seminar.

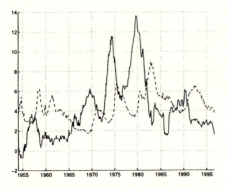

**Figure 1.2.** Monthly unemployment rate (white males over 20 years, dotted line) and monthly inflation rate (CPI, all items, solid line).

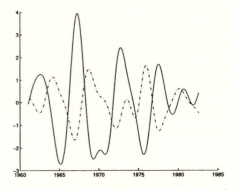

**Figure 1.3.** Business cycle components of monthly unemployment rate (white males over 20 years, dotted line) and monthly inflation rate (CPI, all items, solid line). These components were extracted using the bandpass filters described by Baxter and King.

has been implemented by using the finite-lag bandpass filter described by Baxter and King (1995).[14]

Figure 1.4 plots monthly inflation against monthly unemployment for the subperiod that interests us most, and Figure 1.5 plots the business cycle components of these two series. A comparison of the two figures indicates how focusing on the business-cycle components sharpens the apparent Phillips curve. Figure 1.5 reveals Phillips loops.

---

[14] We set Baxter and King's minimum frequency at 24 months, the maximum at 84 months, and the lag-lead truncation parameter at 84.

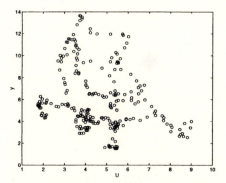

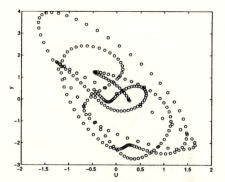

**Figure 1.4.** Scatter plot of monthly inflation (coordinate axis) against white male unemployment (ordinate), 1960–1982.

**Figure 1.5.** Scatter plot of business cycle components of inflation (coordinate axis) against white male unemployent (ordinate), 1960-1982.

*Demographic adjustment and drift*

In Chapter 9, I use these data to estimate an adaptive model of policy making. I adjust for demographic change by choosing a specific unemployment data set. A broader definition of unemployment would put additional low frequency demographic-shift components into the data. Those might be captured by using a unit root process with small innovation variance to drive the unemployment rate. This essay puts a unit root in the inflation-unemployment process from a different source: the drifting beliefs of a monetary authority cut loose from the discipline of Bretton Woods.

## 2
## *Ignoring the Lucas Critique*

### *The Lucas critique*

This essay resurrects econometric and policy evaluation procedures that Lucas decisively criticized. I emphasize a neglected aspect of Lucas's Critique: drifting coefficients. In the adaptive models below, the government ignores the Critique. The government's econometric and policy procedures make coefficients drift, which in turn affects outcomes.

### *Outline*

An econometric model is a collection of stochastic difference equations, parts of which describe private agents' behavior rules for setting prices and quantities. Econometric policy evaluation in the Tinbergen-Theil tradition fixes those parts and superimposes an objective function that orders government preferences over sequences of macroeconomic outcomes. The Tinbergen-Theil government rule maximizes that objective function.

This procedure holds private agents' behavior rules fixed while the government considers variations of its rule. Lucas noted that if private agents solve intertemporal optimization problems, then their decision rules depend on the government's behavior rule.

Because it misses the dependence of the some of the constraints (i.e., parts of the econometric model) on the government's choice, the Tinbergen-Theil formulation incorrectly translates the government's preference over macroeconomic outcomes into an ordering over government decision rules. Therefore, it will not give reliable policy advice. Lucas warned that the Tinbergen-Theil method would not produce the outcomes it promised.[1]

## The appeal to drifting coefficients

Lucas wrote the Critique when Keynesian macroeconometric models were highly regarded as tools for quantitative policy evaluation. The models were being refined to enhance their fits to historical data and their forecasting accuracy. Lucas conceded the impressive forecasting records of Keynesian econometric models, while arguing that good forecasting provided no evidence for the invariance under policy intervention assumed by Tinbergen-Theil. He stressed that typical econometric forecasting practice belied the invariance assumption by frequently adjusting constant terms in important equations. He interpreted those adjustments as approximating Cooley and Prescott's (1973) adaptive coefficients model, and imputed much of the forecasting success to them. The intertemporal instability of estimated relationships, presumably even under stable operating rules for government policy, undermined treating the relationships as invariant with respect to systematic changes in those operating rules.

Lucas raised the issue of parameter drift to distinguish praise for Keynesian econometric models as unconditional[2] forecasting tools from his judgment that they are not suitable for quantitative policy evaluation. However, he did not interpret the observed intertemporal coefficient drift as confirming the theoretical principle that the econometric decision rules of private agents would vary across economies with different government

[1] Lucas and Sargent (1981) gave in to the temptation to say 'I told you so', noting that instead of the of (4, 4) unemployment-inflation rate pair promised by econometric models of the late 1960's, in the late 1970's the U. S. attained (10, 10).

[2] For some reason, the Keynesian econometric literature referred to expectations, conditioned on an observed history, as unconditional forecasts. Unconditional forecasts thus corresponded to conditional expectations. The term conditional forecast meant conditioning on an assumed path of future policy variables.

decision rules. Indeed, each of Lucas's three examples compared hypothetical outcomes across different stationary environments indexed by decision rules for government policy. These examples are silent about drifting coefficients.[3]

*A loose end*

Lucas left the drift in coefficients unexplained. Neither the macroeconomic theory nor the rational expectations econometrics constructed after Lucas's Critique explains such drift. Each of these traditions focused on environments with time-invariant transition functions. Observations drawn from rational expectations equilibria for such environments would not provide significant evidence of parameter drift, even for misspecified models.[4],[5] As emphasized in Chapter 7, such stationary environments are general enough to comprehend governments that choose policy in the erroneous way that Lucas criticized.

Yet coefficients continue to drift for macroeconometric models. Forecasting methods based on vector autoregressions incorporate explicit priors in the form of stochastic laws of motion for the coefficients.[6] The literature on unit roots in macroeconomics also can be interpreted as modeling drifting constants. Thus, the forecasting literature has taken coefficient drift increasingly seriously, but with little help from the rational expectations

[3] Lucas (1972) and Sargent (1971) described a test for the predicted outcome–policy rule dependence. That test does not use a random coefficients model. I recall that many early readers of Lucas's Critique misunderstood his reference to drifting coefficients as supporting his basic theoretical point.

[4] See Halbert White (1982), Sims (1993), and Hansen and Sargent (1993) for studies of classes of specification errors in stationary stochastic environments.

[5] See the discussion in Chapter 8 about how random-coefficients models are consistent with stationarity. Interpreting evidence of coefficient drift as evidence of model misspecification requires an alternative model that somehow causes the moments used in constructing estimators to depend on calendar time in a detectable way.

[6] See Doan, Litterman, and Sims (1984) and the RATS manual.

tradition. Like Lucas's Critique, the econometric forecasting literature typically offers no economic explanation for parameter drift, but it seeks to account for and exploit it in making forecasts.

*Parameter drift as point of departure*

I start with parameter drift, treating it as a smoking gun. It is the key piece of evidence that the government's beliefs about the economy and therefore its policy toward inflation have evolved over time. I form a model from two main components: a Tinbergen-Theil theory of government decision making (the Phelps problem discussed in Chapter 5); and a drifting-coefficients econometric procedure for the government that features the constant adjustments that Lucas wrote about. I study the quality of the outcomes that these policy procedures produce and compare them with historical outcomes and also with what would occur under rational expectations. I constrain the exercise by assuming that a rational expectations version of the natural-rate hypothesis is true. I do not examine unusual supply shocks and other plausible explanations of post-World War II U. S. inflation.

## Relevance of the critique

In focusing on the government's learning behavior, I raise an issue discussed by Sargent and Wallace (1976), Sims (1982), and Sargent (1983) in the wake of Lucas's Critique. If the fundamentals of the environment are time-invariant (e.g., they are described by a stationary stochastic process), the forces underlying consistency proofs in econometrics cause the government's econometric estimates and its decision rule to converge.[7] In the limit, there can emerge a self-confirming equilibrium, where the government's estimates of its econometric model are reinforced

---

[7] The standard econometric proofs of consistency must be altered along lines described by Bray and Savin (1986) and Marcet and Sargent (1989a, 1989b).

jointly by its own behavior and the private sector's reactions to it.

Within a self-confirming equilibrium, the relevance of some aspects of the Lucas Critique vanish. First, although the invariance under intervention assumption used in the government's decision problem is wrong, the government is not disappointed in outcomes because they are statistically consistent with its beliefs.

Second, in addition to imposing rational expectations for private agents, a self-confirming equilibrium restricts the government's econometric model and its behavior. Free parameters describing the government's behavior disappear, thereby eliminating regime changes as an object of analysis. Sims (1982) implicitly appeals to a self-confirming equilibrium when he argues that regime changes are rare because existing policies are approximately optimal. Thus, a self-confirming equilibrium is a rational expectations equilibrium but one with fewer parameters than those in the models of Lucas (1972, 1976), which had parameters describing government policy. We would need those lost parameters to represent regime changes.[8], [9]

Third, to admit regime changes and drifting coefficients, convergence to a self-confirming equilibrium must be resisted. I arrest convergence by exchanging the government's least squares for an adaptive-coefficients algorithm like Cooley and Prescott's (1973). The adaptive-coefficients algorithm endows the government with a suspicion that the environment is unstable, which makes it overweight recent observations relative to least squares. This weakens the tendency of the economy to converge to a self-confirming equilibrium by strengthening a source of sustained dynamics along an escape route. Regime changes occur along the escape route.

---

[8]  For the same reasons, Lucas and Stokey (1983) is not about regime changes.
[9]  In 'The Ends of Four Big Inflations' (Sargent (1986)), I interpreted data from hyperinflations and their terminations in the Lucas (1972, 1976) tradition by shifting free parameters indexing the government's monetary-fiscal policies.

## *Rational expectations models*

Ironically, the procedures that violate the Lucas Critique yield better outcomes than ones that respect it. To expand on this point, I begin by reviewing the kinds of models and procedures that respect the Critique. To summarize important developments in macroeconomic thinking from the 1980's and early 1990's, the next two chapters apply the Nash equilibrium concept to a model with a natural unemployment rate. The theory in these chapters carries through the vision of Sims (1982) that macroeconomic observations reflect purposeful and knowledgeable behavior by both the government and the private sector. These models prompt us to examine what we mean by regime changes.

The rational expectations models in the next two chapters respect the Lucas Critique. Models that challenge and extend the Lucas Critique appear later.

# 3
## The Credibility Problem

### Introduction

This chapter describes the basic expectational Phillips curve model, modifications of which underlie both story lines. The following chapter sets out a repeated economy version of this model. Together, these two chapters formalize the temptation to inflate unleashed by the discovery of the Phillips curve, the value of a commitment technology for resisting that temptation, and the fragility of reputational mechanisms as substitutes for commitment. Despite aliases, rational expectations is the only equilibrium concept throughout. Alterations in the timing of actors' decisions induce different economies with distinct outcomes.

These two chapters summarize rational expectations benchmarks that form the point of departure for the adaptive expectations models that follow. The concluding section of the next chapter offers my opinion of how faithfully this benchmark theory supports the triumph of natural-rate theory as an interpretation of history.

### One-period economy

A government faces a credibility problem whenever it wishes to make decisions sooner than it must. Comparing outcomes under two different timing protocols reveals a credibility problem. In one, by choosing before the private sector, the government takes into account its effects on private decisions. In the other, the government decides after the private sector. The deterioration in outcomes under the second timing protocol measures the loss from the inability to commit.

Though credibility problems are intrinsically dynamic, it is possible to describe them in the context of a one-period model under different patterns of within period timing. This way of introducing the credibility problem prepares the way for multi-period analyses. I describe a version of the one-period model of Kydland and Prescott in Stokey's (1989, 1990) terms.

A government chooses a $y \in Y$. There is a continuum of private agents, each of whom sets $\xi$, its expectation about $y$. The average setting of $\xi$ is $x$. To capture that each private agent solves a forecasting problem, define the one period payoff function of a private agent as

$$u(\xi, x, y) = -.5[(y - \xi)^2 + y^2].  \tag{1}$$

Given $y$, each private agent maximizes its payoff (solves its forecasting problem) by setting $\xi = y$. Since all private agents face the same problem, $x = \xi$. We require that $y \in Y$, $\xi \in X \equiv Y$, $x \in Y$. In our analysis of credible government policies, we shall make $Y$ a compact subset of the real line.

To implement Kydland and Prescott's example, let $(U, y, x)$ be the unemployment rate, the inflation rate, and the public's expectation of the inflation rate, respectively. The government's one-period payoff is

$$-.5(U^2 + y^2).  \tag{2}$$

Unemployment is determined by an expectations augmented Phillips curve[1]

$$U = U^* - \theta(y - x), \quad \theta > 0.  \tag{3}$$

The equation asserts that unemployment deviates from $U^*$, the natural-rate, only when there is surprise inflation or deflation.

---

[1] In 1973, Lucas used this parametric Phillips curve to approximate the restrictions that his 1972 model placed on time series of unemployment and inflation.

Substituting (3) into (2) lets us express the government's pay-off as a function $r(x, y)$ defined as

$$r(x, y) = -.5[(U^* - \theta(y - x))^2 + y^2].  \qquad (4)$$

We work with the following objects.

RATIONAL EXPECTATIONS EQUILIBRIUM: A triple $(U, x, y)$ satisfying (3) and $y = x$.

GOVERNMENT (ONE-PERIOD) BEST RESPONSE: Given the public's expectation $x$, a decision rule $B(x) = \arg\max_y r(x, y)$ for setting $y$.

NASH EQUILIBRIUM: A pair $(x, y)$ satisfying (i) $x = y$, and (ii) $y = B(x)$.

RAMSEY PROBLEM: $\max_y r(y, y)$. The *Ramsey outcome* is the value of $y$ that attains the maximum.

BEST RESPONSE DYNAMICS: The dynamical system $y_t = B(y_{t-1})$, $y_0 \in Y$.

A rational expectations equilibrium is a $U, x, y$ triple that lies on the Phillips curve, and for which private agents are solving their forecasting problem (i.e., they are not fooled), given $x$. Substituting $x = y$ into the Phillips curve (3) shows that $U = U^*$ in any rational expectations equilibrium. This identifies $U^*$ as the natural unemployment rate.

A Nash equilibrium builds in a best response by the government, taking the state of expectations $x$ as given, and also a response $x = y$ by the market, i.e., rational expectations for a given $y$. The government's best response function is

$$y = B(x) = \frac{\theta}{\theta^2 + 1} U^* + \frac{\theta^2}{\theta^2 + 1} x.  \qquad (5)$$

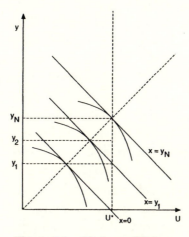

**Figure 3.1.** Nash equilibrium, Ramsey outcome, and best response dynamics.

The Nash equilibrium is $y^N = x^N = \theta U, U = U^*$. The Ramsey outcome is $y^R = x^R = 0, U = U^*$. Thus, $r(x^R, y^R) = -.5U^{*2}$ and $r(x^N, y^N) = -.5(1 + \theta^2)U^{*2}$.

The Nash equilibrium is supported by a timing protocol in which the government decides after the private sector sets its expectations. The Ramsey equilibrium is associated with a timing protocol in which the government chooses first, knowing that it is manipulating the private sector's expectations, because $y = x$ in a rational expectations equilibrium.

Figure 3.1 depicts the Nash equilibrium outcome and the Ramsey outcome when $\theta = 1$. Solid lines depict a family of Phillips curves for different levels of expected inflation $x$, with slope $\theta = -1$; curves are drawn for $x = 0, y_1, y^N$. The Nash equilibrium outcome is $(U^*, y^N)$. The Ramsey outcome is $(U^*, 0)$. The government's best response setting for $y$, given $x$, occurs at the tangency of an indifference equation induced by (2) with the Phillips curve indexed by $x$.

Figure 3.2 depicts the best response function. Given that the public expects inflation $x$, the government's best one-period action is to set $y = B(x)$. A Nash equilibrium occurs where $y = x = B(x)$, i.e., where $B(x)$ intersects the 45 degree line. Best response dynamics convert the one-period model into a dynamic one by positing an adaptive mechanism by which $x$ depends on the observed history of $y$, namely, $x_t = y_{t-1}$. This leads to the dynamics $y_t = B(y_{t-1})$ depicted in Figure 3.1. Let the system start out with $x = 0$. Then the government sets $y = y_1$. This provokes the public to set $x = y_1$, leading the government to reset $y = y_2$. The limit of this process is evidently $y = y^N$, $x = y^N$, a self-confirming situation. Thus, best response dynamics converge to a Nash equilibrium, and reinforce $(U^*, y^N)$ as the prediction of the model without a government commitment technology.

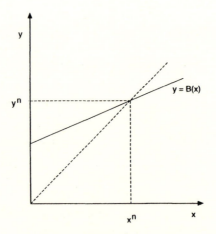

**Figure 3.2.**   The government's best response function, $B(x)$.

A version of these best response dynamics also emerges from least squares learning.

*Least squares learning converges to Nash*

Least-squares learning plays a key role in this essay. The present example introduces analytical elements of least squares learning in self-referential systems, elements that reappear later in more complex settings. Least-squares learning can, like best response dynamics, converge to the Nash equilibrium outcome.

Margaret Bray (1982) studied convergence to rational expectations equilibrium of a competitive market with a one-period supply response lag in which traders formed the expected price by averaging past ones. In the same spirit, for integer $t \geq 2$, assume that $x_t$ is the average of past $y_t$'s, so $x_t = (t-1)^{-1} \sum_{s=1}^{t-1} y_s$. Represent $x_t$ recursively

$$x_t = x_{t-1} + (t-1)^{-1}(y_{t-1} - x_{t-1}), \qquad (6)$$

where $x_1 = 0$. Assume that actual $y_t$ is formed from a disturbed version of the best response mapping evaluated at $x_t$:

$$y_t = B(x_t) + \eta_t. \qquad (7)$$

Here $\eta_t$ is an independent and identically distributed random term with mean zero, included to represent the government's imperfect control of inflation. Substituting (6) into (7) gives

$$x_t = x_{t-1} + (t-1)^{-1} \left[ B(x_{t-1}) - x_{t-1} + \eta_t \right]. \qquad (8)$$

By applying the theory of stochastic approximation, we show that the limiting behavior of $x_t$ emerging from (8) is described by an associated differential equation[2]

$$\frac{dx}{dt} = B(x) - x. \qquad (9)$$

---

[2] The ordinary differential equation is formed mechanically by setting $\frac{d}{dt}x = E\left[B(x) - x + \eta\right]$, where $E$ is the mathematical expectation over the unconditional distribution of $\eta$, evaluated at a fixed $x$.

The rest point of this differential equation evidently satisfies $x = B(x)$, which makes it the Nash equilibrium inflation rate $x = \theta U^*$. The linearity of the best response mapping (5) makes the ordinary differential equation (the ODE ) (9) linear. Define $\mathcal{M} = \frac{d}{dx}(B(x) - x)$. Evidently, $\mathcal{M} = B'(x) - 1 = -\frac{1}{\theta^2+1}$. Because $\mathcal{M} < 0$, the ODE is stable about the rest point. This brings to bear theorems described by Marcet and Sargent (1989a) that supply conditions under which the convergence of $x_t$ to $y^N$ occurs globally.[3] The appendix to this chapter contains an introduction to stochastic approximation.

Thus, the least squares dynamics confirm the pessimism of the best response dynamics. This pessimism undermines the triumph of natural-rate theory story, especially the triumph aspect. Given an initial condition in the form of a gold standard or Bretton Woods value of $x$, the best response or least squares dynamics can explain the acceleration of inflation observed in figure 1.1. But they cannot explain the stabilization that Volcker engineered.

Later I reformulate versions of least squares learning in ways designed to moderate this pessimism. But this will move us away from the triumph and toward the vindication story.

---

[3] See Marcet and Sargent (1995) and Evans and Honkapohja (1998b) for discussions linking $\mathcal{M}$ also to the rate of convergence of $x$ to $x^N$. A necessary condition for convergence at the typical rate of $t^{.5}$ is that $\mathcal{M} < -.5$. When $\mathcal{M} \in [-.5, 0)$, $x_t$ converges to $x^N$ but at a slower rate governed by the absolute value of $\mathcal{M}$. See Chen (1993) and Chen and White (1993) for some results on rates of convergence for nonparametric recursive algorithms.

*More foresight*

Best response and least squares are out of equilibrium dynamics tacked on to a one-period economy. They force all movement through expectation formation.[4] In choosing inflation, the government forgets that the economy lasts for more than one period.

Better outcomes can occur if the government plans for the future. In subsequent chapters, I describe three different ways of modeling foresight. These impute varying amounts of rationality and predict different qualities of outcomes. The first draws from the literature on reputation or sustainable plans and attributes rational expectations to both the government and the public. This setting either confirms the pessimism emerging from Kydland and Prescott's analysis or replaces it with agnosticism: many outcomes are sustainable, ranging from repetition of the Ramsey outcome to paths much worse than repetition of the one-period Nash outcome.

A second keeps the government rational but gives the public adaptive expectations in the original Friedman–Cagan sense.[5] Depending on a comparison between a discount factor and an adaptation parameter, this setup can improve outcomes and possibly sustain repetition of the Ramsey outcome.

A third attributes adaptive behavior to both the government and the public. The outcomes depend on details of the beliefs assigned to the government. A vindication of econometric policy evaluation can emerge.

---

[4] The only state variable measures the public's expectations.

[5] By adopting the Cagan-Friedman specification, we will restrict the strategy space in a way to limit the set of outcomes far below those found in Chapter 4.

## *Appendix on stochastic approximation*

An argument of Kushner and Clark (1978) shows that the ODE governs the tail behavior of the original stochastic difference equation (6). The two key components are a shift in time scale and a liberal application of averaging.

For $n \geq 0$, let $\{a_n\}_{n=0}^{\infty}$ be a positive sequence of real scalars obeying $\lim_{n \to \infty} a_n = 0, \sum_n a_n = +\infty, \sum_n a_n^2 < +\infty$. As an example, $a_n = \frac{1}{n+1}$ satisfies these assumptions. Rewrite (6) as

$$x_{n+1} = x_n + a_n \left[ B(x_n) - x_n + \eta_n \right], \qquad (10)$$

where again $\eta_n$ is an independent and identically distributed process with mean zero and finite variance. To deduce the differential equation associated with the stochastic difference equation (10), we work with the transformed time scale $t_0 = 0$, $t_n = \sum_{i=0}^{n-1} a_i$. Our strategy will be to represent the solution of the difference equation (10) as a distributed lag, to transform the time scale from $n$ to $t_n$, and then to interpolate the solution from the discrete points $t_n, n \geq 0$ to $t \geq 0, t \in I\!\!R$. In working with the extension to positive real $t$'s, it will be convenient to use the mapping $m(t) = \max\{n : t_n \leq t\}$, which serves as an inverse mapping from $t$ back to the original units of time $n$.

For $n \geq 0$, let $x^0(t_n)$ denote the solution of (10) with initial condition $x^0(0)$ at $n = 0$. Recursions on (10) yield

$$x^0(t_n) = x^0(0) + \sum_{i=0}^{n-1} a_i \left[ B(x(t_i)) - x(t_i) \right] + \sum_{i=0}^{n-1} a_i \eta_i. \qquad (11)$$

Following Kushner and Clark (1978), define piecewise-linear interpolated values of $x^0(t)$ for $t \in I\!\!R, t \geq 0$, by $x^0(t_n) = x_n$ and

$$x^0(t) = \frac{t_{n+1} - t}{a_n} x_n + \frac{t - t_n}{a_n} x_{n+1}, \quad t \in (t_n, t_{n+1}).$$

Define the piecewise-linear interpolated values $\eta^0(t)$ in an analogous fashion. The interpolated $x^0(t)$ is evidently a continuous-time stochastic process.

Kushner and Clark use the distributed lag representation of the solution (11), which is exact at the original points $t_n$, to motivate approximation of $x^0(t)$ by the integral equation

$$x^0(t) = x^0(0) + \int_0^t \left[ B(x^0(s)) - x^0(s) \right] ds + R(t), \qquad (12)$$

where $R(t)$ is an approximation error constructed by subtracting the rest of the right side of (12) from the right side of (11). The approximation error $R(t)$ evidently has two components, one associated with approximating the distributed lag in $B(x) - x$ with an integral; the other with the distributed lag in $\eta_s$ in (11). Kushner and Clark want somehow to drive each of these components and therefore the approximation error $R$ to zero.

This is not possible for small $t$, but it is for a large enough $t$. Kushner and Clark work with a sequence of left-shifted versions of (11). In particular, they define the $n$th left-shifted process

$$\begin{aligned} x^n(t) &= x^0(t + t_n), \quad t \geq -t_n \\ x^n(t) &= x^0(0), \quad t \leq -t_n. \end{aligned} \qquad (13)$$

The left-shifted process can be represented as

$$x^n(t) = x^n(0) + \int_0^t \left[ B(x^n(s)) - x^n(s) \right] ds + W_n(t) + R^n(t), \quad (14)$$

where

$$W_n(t) = \sum_{i=n}^{m(t_n+t)} a_i \eta_i, \qquad (15)$$

and where $R^n(t)$ equals the difference between an interpolant of a distributed lag in $B(x) - x$ and the integral.

Kushner and Clark display technical conditions under which the two approximation errors $W_n(t)$ and $R^n(t)$ can be driven to zero as $n \rightarrow +\infty$. The key in making the random process $W_n(t)$ converge to zero is to note that it is a martingale sequence with variance $\operatorname{var}(\eta) \sum_{i=n}^{m(t_n+t)} a_i^2$ which by virtue of the assumption that $\sum_{i=0}^{\infty} a_i^2 < +\infty$ approaches zero as $n \to \infty$. The term $R^n(t)$ is sent to zero by making $a_i \to 0$ as $i \to \infty$, which drives to zero the norm of the mesh of the term $\sum_{i=0}^{N-1} a_{i+n} \left[ B(x^n(t_i)) - x^n(t_i) \right]$ used to approximate the integral.[6]

By studying the limit as $n \to 0$ of the sequence of left-shifted processes in (14), Kushner and Clark establish that the limiting behavior of the original stochastic difference equation (10) is shared by the non-stochastic integral equation

$$\tilde{x}(t) = \tilde{x}(0) + \int_0^t B(\tilde{x}(s)) - \tilde{x}(s))d\,s. \tag{16}$$

Differentiating gives the ODE

$$\frac{d}{dt}\tilde{x}(t) = B(\tilde{x}(t)) - \tilde{x}(t). \tag{17}$$

Equation (16) or (17) is said to describe the mean dynamics of the original system (10).

Later we will study systems like (10) in which $a_i$ does not approach zero as $i$ grows.

---

[6] Note that $\{a\}_{i+n}^{N-1}$ is serving as the partition of the $x$-axis in the Riemann-Stieljes approximation to the integral.

# 4
## Credible Government Policies

### Perfection

This chapter uses Kydland and Prescott's example to convey the theory of sustainable or credible government policies. We examine whether this theory can moderate or extend the pessimism from Kydland and Prescott's analysis.[1] My conclusion is that the multiplicity of credible plans replaces pessimism with agnosticism. The theory described in this chapter is difficult if a reader has not seen it before. A reader who is not interested in the theory of credible policy will loose little of the flow of the main argument in this book if he accepts my judgment on the meaning of this literature and skips to chapter 5 at this point.

The economy repeats itself for each $t \geq 1$. In this section, we let $Y = [0, y^{\#}]$. The lowest possible setting of the inflation rate is the Ramsey outcome $0$. The upper bound on inflation $y^{\#}$ makes the government's problem non-trivial. The government evaluates outcome paths $(x, y) \equiv \{x_t, y_t\}_{t=1}^{\infty}$ according to

$$V^g(x, y) = (1 - \delta) \sum_{t=1}^{\infty} \delta^{t-1} r(x_t, y_t), \quad \delta \in (0, 1). \qquad (18)$$

The government uses a strategy with a recursive representation. This substantially restricts the space of strategies because most history-dependent strategies cannot be represented recursively.

[1] For descriptions of theories of credible government policy see Chari and Kehoe (1990), Stokey (1989, 1991), Rogoff (1989), and Chari, Kehoe, and Prescott (1989). For applications of the framework of Abreu, Pearce, and Stacchetti, see Chang (1998), Phelan and Stacchetti (1998), and Ljungqvist and Sargent (1998, chapter 7).

Nevertheless, this class of strategies excludes no equilibrium payoffs $V^g$. We use the following:

DEFINITION: A *recursive government strategy* is a pair of functions $\sigma = (\sigma_1, \sigma_2)$ and an initial condition $v_1$ with the following structure:

$$v_1 \in I\!R \text{ is given;}$$

$$y_t = \sigma_1(v_t); \text{ and} \tag{19}$$

$$v_{t+1} = \sigma_2(v_t, x_t, y_t),$$

where $v_t$ is a state variable designed to summarize the history of outcomes before $t$.

This form of strategy operates much like an autoregression to let the government's choice $y_t$ depend on the history $\{y_s, x_s\}_{s=1}^{t-1}$, as mediated through the state variable $v_t$. Representation (19) induces history-dependent government policies, and thereby allows for reputation. We shall soon see that beyond its role in tracking histories, $v_t$ also summarizes the future.[2]

Each member of the private sector forms an expectation about the government's action according to

$$x_t = \sigma_1(v_t), \tag{20}$$

where $v_t$ is known to each private agent. Equation (20) builds in rational expectations, because the private sector knows both the state variable $v_t$ and the government's decision rule $\sigma$.

A strategy $(\sigma, v_1)$ recursively generates an entire outcome path expressed as $(x, y) = (x, y)(\sigma, v_1)$. By substituting the outcome path into (18), we find that strategy $(\sigma, v_1)$ induces a value for the government, which we write as

$$V^g\big((x,y)(\sigma, v)\big) = V^g(\sigma, v). \tag{21}$$

---

[2] By iterating (19), we can construct a sequence of functions indexed by $t \geq 1$ $\{\sigma_{3t}(h_t)\}$, mapping histories that are augmented by initial conditions $h_t = (\{x_s, y_s\}_{s=1}^{t-1}, v_1)$ into government time-$t$ actions $y_t \in Y$. A strategy for the repeated economy is a sequence of such functions without the restriction that it have a recursive representation.

So far, we have not interpreted the state variable $v$, except as a particular measure of the history of outcomes. The theory of credible policy ties past and future together by making the state variable $v$ a promised value, an outcome to be expressed:

$$v = V^g(\sigma, v). \tag{22}$$

Equations (19), (20), (21), and (22) assert a dual role for $v$. In (19), $v$ accounts for past outcomes. In equations (21) and (22), $v$ looks forward. The state $v_t$ is a discounted future value with which the government enters time $t$ based on past outcomes. Depending on the outcome $y$ and the entering promised value $v$, $\sigma_2$ updates the promised value with which the government leaves the period. The strategy gives current and future outcomes that make the government choose as expected. We postpone struggling with which of two valid interpretations of the government's strategy should be emphasized: something chosen by the government, or a description of a system of public expectations to which the government conforms.

### Historical antecedents

Credibility means public awareness that each period the government wants to execute its plans. Formalizing the idea of credibility was an important achievement from the 1980's, although a sophisticated understanding of credibility existed as early as the 1780's. The great finance minister Jacques Necker used this idea to explain to King Louis XVI why it was difficult for him to borrow more even though he was nominally an absolute monarch. After reminding him how 18th century French institutions limited his power to raise taxes but left him free to renege on debt payments, in 1784 Necker told the King:[3]

'Therefore one can rekindle or sustain public trust only by giving reassurances on the sovereign's intentions, and

---

[3] This quotation is part of a longer passage cited by Sargent and Velde (1995).

by proving that no motive can incite him to fail his obligations.'

The formal definition of a subgame perfect equilibrium builds
in every aspect of Necker's sentence. A king could prove that he
would never fail his obligations by never wanting to fail them;
that is, by conforming to a forecasting scheme that incorporates
his incentive constraints. These incentive constraints assure that
at each time and with each contingency, the King's current payoff
plus continuation value would be higher if he confirmed those
expectations than if he did not. Necker expresses frustration
over the role of French institutions in making his sovereign's
debt problem worse than it could be under improved institutions. The King could not choose his own behavior rule.[4]

These ideas are reflected in the following definition:

DEFINITION: A recursive strategy (19) with promised value $v$ is a
subgame perfect equilibrium (SPE) if and only if (a) $\sigma_2(v, \sigma_1(v), \eta)$
is a value for a subgame perfect equilibrium $\forall \eta \in Y$; and (b)

$$
\begin{aligned}
v &= (1 - \delta)r(\sigma_1(v), \sigma_1(v)) + \delta\sigma_2(v, \sigma_1(v), \sigma_1(v)) \\
&\geq (1 - \delta)r(\sigma_1(v), \eta) + \delta\sigma_2(v, \sigma_1(v), \eta), \quad \forall \eta \in Y.
\end{aligned}
\tag{23}
$$

Conditions (a) and (b) associate with a subgame perfect equilibrium four objects: a promised value $v$; a first-period out-
come pair $(y, y)$, where $y = \sigma_1(v)$; a continuation value $v' = \sigma_2(v, \sigma_1(v), \sigma_1(v))$ if the required first-period outcome is observed;
and another continuation value $\tilde{v} = \sigma_2(v, \sigma_1(v), \eta)$ if the required
first-period outcome is not observed. All of the continuation
values must themselves be attained with subgame perfect equilibria. In terms of these objects, (b) is an incentive constraint

---

[4] The King was complaining about an expectations trap; see Chari, Christiano,
and Eichenbaum (1998).

inspiring the government to adhere to the equilibrium:

$$v = (1 - \delta)r(y, y) + \delta v'$$
$$\geq (1 - \delta)r(y, \eta) + \delta \tilde{v}, \quad \forall \eta \in Y.$$

This states that the government receives more if it adheres to an action called for by its strategy than if it departs. Part (a) of the definition requires that the continuation values be values for subgame perfect equilibria. The definition is circular, because the same class of objects, namely equilibrium values $v$, occur on each side of (23). Circularity comes with recursivity.

Abreu, Pearce, and Stacchetti (APS) (1986, 1990) showed how recursive equilibria of form (19) can attain all subgame perfect equilibrium values. APS's innovation was to shift the focus away from the set of equilibrium strategies and toward the set of values $V$ attainable with subgame equilibrium strategies. They described a set $V$ such that for all $v \in V$, $v$ is the value associated with a subgame perfect equilibrium. APS developed a recursive algorithm for computing the set $V$.

*The method of Abreu-Pearce-Stacchetti*

Dynamic programming solves single-agent recursive optimization problems by finding an optimal value function. The optimal value function is computed by iterating on the Bellman equation, which maps continuation values giving tomorrow's discounted value as a function of tomorrow's state variables into today's discounted value as a function of today's state variables. The mapping from continuation values to current values embodies the backward induction of dynamic programming. Iterations on the Bellman equation converge to make continuation value (functions) equal value (functions).[5]

---

[5] It is helpful to indicate this structure within John McCall's celebrated model of sequential labor market search. In the McCall model, each period an unemployed worker receives an offer to work forever at a wage $w$ drawn from the same distribution with cumulative density function $F(w)$. While unemployed,

APS adapted dynamic programming to characterize the set of equilibrium values in terms of an operator mapping sets of continuation values into sets of values. They computed the set of equilibrium values by iterating to convergence on that operator. Their method starts with a candidate set $W \subset \mathbb{R}$, where any $w \in W$ can be assigned as a continuation value for adhering to or for deviating from the recommendation of the strategy. The idea is to start with a large but bounded set $W$,[6] then to select a first period rational expectations outcome $(y, y)$ and two associated continuation values drawn from $W$, a $w_1$ for adhering to $(y, y)$, and a $w_2$ associated with deviating from $(y, y)$.[7] The candidate continuation value $w_1$ must be high enough, and $w_2$ low enough, to make the government want to adhere to $(y, y)$, given those continuation values. Out of the two continuation values $w_1, w_2 \in W \times W$, this construction produces

the worker receives $c$ in unemployment compensation. The worker wants to maximize his expected discounted income, with discount factor $\delta \in (0, 1)$, where income equals $c$ if unemployed, and the wage $w$ if employed. Once he accepts a job, the worker stays in it forever. Let $v$ be the optimal value of this problem for an unemployed worker who is about to draw an offer for this period. The Bellman equation for this problem is

$$v = \int_w \max \left\{ \frac{w}{1 - \delta}, \delta v + c \right\} d\,F(w).$$

Letting $T(v)$ be the function defined on the right side, this equation can be expressed as the fixed point

$$v = T(v).$$

The fixed point can be computed by iterating to convergence on

$$v_{j+1} = T(v_j),$$

starting from $v_0 = 0$. Here $T$ maps a continuation value $v_j$ into a current value $v_{j+1}$. This iteration does backward induction.

[6] The set has to be bounded because with an unbounded set of prospective continuation values, any value could seemingly be supported; but there would exist no associated outcome path that could attain it via equation (18).

[7] Remember that a rational expectations outcome is $(y, y)$ because the private sector knows the government's strategy.

a value $w$ satisfying $w = (1 - \delta)r(y, y) + \delta w_1 \geq (1 - \delta)r(y, \eta) + \delta w_2$, $\forall \eta \in Y$. Thus, the operator produces candidate values from candidate continuation values.

The construction of values out of continuation values includes the incentive constraints imposed in condition (b) of the definition of a subgame perfect equilibrium, but it ignores condition (a) because the continuation values are arbitrary. APS thus conceive an operator $B$ that maps an arbitrary compact set of potential continuation values into a set of values. They let $B(W)$ denote this set.

To find subgame perfect equilibrium values, condition (a) of the definition must be incorporated. The challenge is to guarantee that each continuation value comes from a SPE and thus to assure that the set of subgame equilibrium values $V$ satisfies $V = B(V)$. This expresses that subgame perfect equilibrium values are supported by subgame perfect equilibrium continuation values. The set $V$ is a fixed point of the operator $B$ mapping continuation values to values. APS showed that $V$ is the largest fixed point of $B$ and how it can be computed by iterating on $B$, starting from a large enough initial set $W_0$ of candidate continuation values.

APS use two concepts. Admissibility denotes a value and an associated first period outcome $y$ attainable with an arbitrary set of continuation values. Self-generation is about closure under the $B$ operator.

ADMISSIBILITY: A pair $(y, w)$ is *admissible* with respect to the set of continuation values $W$ if there exist continuation values $w_1, w_2 \in W \times W$ such that $w = (1-\delta)r(y, y)+\delta w_1 \geq (1-\delta)r(y, \eta)+\delta w_2$, $\forall \eta \in Y$.[8]

For an arbitrary set of candidate continuation values $W$, the $B(W)$ operator of APS selects the associated $w$ pieces for all

---

[8] An equivalent definition formally closer to APS's would be to state the definition in terms of the triple $(x, y, w)$ and to add the requirement that $(x, y)$ forms a rational expectations equilibrium.

admissible pairs $(y, w)$. A candidate first-period outcome $y$ is associated with each element $\tilde{w} \in W$.

SELF-GENERATION: The set $W$ of prospective continuation values is *self-generating* if $W \subseteq B(W)$.

Each value in a self-generating set is supported by continuation values drawn from the set. Admissibility builds in feature (b) and self generation builds in feature (a) of the definition of a SPE. It follows that the set of SPE values is self-generating.

Imitating dynamic programming, APS iterate on $B$ to find the largest self-generating set. APS show that: (1) the set of SPE values is the largest self-generating set; (2) $B$ maps compact sets into compact sets; (3) $B$ is monotone, meaning that if $W_2 \subseteq W_1$, then $B(W_2) \subseteq B(W_1)$; and (4) starting from any $W_0$ such that $W_1 = B(W_0) \subseteq W_0$, the algorithm $W_j = B(W_{j-1})$ converges monotonically to $V = B(V)$.

Below we describe another way to find the set of SPE values.

## *Examples of recursive SPE*

To illustrate possible outcomes, I construct several SPE equilibria using a guess and verify technique. First guess $(v_1, \sigma_1, \sigma_2)$ in (19), then verify parts (a) and (b) of the definition of a SPE.

The examples parallel the historical development of the theory. (1) The first example is infinite repetition of a one-period Nash outcome. (2) Barro and Gordon (1982) and Stokey (1989) used the value from infinite repetition of the Nash outcome as a continuation value to deter deviation from the Ramsey outcome. For sufficiently high discount factors, the continuation value associated with repetition of the Nash outcome can deter the government from deviating from infinite repetition of the Ramsey outcome, but not for low discount factors. (3) Abreu (1986) and Stokey (1991) showed that Abreu's 'stick and carrot'

strategy can have a value lower than repetition of the Nash outcome. (4) We display a pair of simple programming problems
to find the best and worst SPE values.

*Infinite repetition of Nash outcome*

It is easy to construct an equilibrium whose outcome path forever repeats the one-period Nash outcome. Let $v^N = r(y^N, y^N)$.
The proposed equilibrium is

$$v_1 = v^N,$$
$$\sigma_1(v_t) = y^N \ \forall \ v_t, \text{ and}$$
$$\sigma_2(v_t, x_t, y_t) = v^N, \ \forall \ (v_t, x_t, y_t).$$

Here for each $t$, $v^N$ simultaneously plays the roles of $v, v'$, and
$\tilde{v}$ in condition (b). Condition (a) is satisfied by construction, and
condition (b) collapses to

$$r(y^N, y^N) \geq r(y^N, B(y^N)),$$

which is satisfied at equality by the definition of a best response
function. The equilibrium outcome forever repeats Kydland
and Prescott's time consistent equilibrium.

*Infinite repetition of a better-than-Nash outcome*

Let $v^b$ be a value associated with outcome $y^b$ such that $v^b =$
$r(y^b, y^b) > v^N$. Suppose further that

$$r(y^b, B(y^b)) - r(y^b, y^b) \leq \frac{\delta}{1-\delta}(v^b - v^N). \tag{24}$$

The left side is the one-period return to the government from deviating from $y^b$; the right side is the difference in present values
associated with conforming to the plan versus reverting forever
to the Nash equilibrium. When the inequality is satisfied, the

equilibrium presents the government with an incentive not to deviate from $y_b$. Then a SPE is

$$v_1 = v^b;$$

$$\sigma_1(v) = \begin{cases} y^b, & \text{if } v = v^b; \\ y^N, & \text{otherwise;} \end{cases}$$

$$\sigma_2(v, x, y) = \begin{cases} v^b, & \text{if } (v, x, y) = (v^b, y^b, y^b); \\ v^N & \text{, otherwise.} \end{cases}$$

This strategy specifies outcome $(y^b, y^b)$ and continuation value $v^b$ so long as $v^b$ is the value promised at the beginning of the period. Any deviation from $y^b$ generates continuation value $v^N$. Inequality (24) validates condition (b) of the definition of SPE.

Barro and Gordon (1982) considered a version of this equilibrium in which (24) is satisfied with $v^b = v^R, y^b = y^R$. In this case, anticipated reversion to Nash forever supports Ramsey forever. When (24) is *not* satisfied for $v^b = v^R, y = y^R$, we can solve for the best SPE value $\tilde{v}$ supportable by infinite reversion to Nash (with associated action $\tilde{y}$) from

$$\tilde{v} = r(\tilde{y}, \tilde{y}) = (1 - \delta)r(\tilde{y}, B(\tilde{y})) + \delta v^N > v^N. \tag{25}$$

The payoff from following the strategy equals that from deviating and reverting to Nash. Any value lower than this can be supported, but none higher.

In a related context, Abreu (1986) searched for a way to support something better than $v^b$ when $v^b < v^R$. First, one must construct an equilibrium that yields a value worse than permanent repetition of the Nash outcome. The expectation of reverting to this equilibrium supports something better than $v^b$ in (25).

Somehow the government must be induced temporarily to generate inflation higher than the Nash outcome, meaning that the government is tempted to lower the inflation rate. An equilibrium system of expectations has to be constructed that makes the government expect to do better in the future only by conforming to expectations that it temporarily generate higher inflation than the Nash level.

*Something worse: a stick and carrot strategy*

We want a continuation value $v^*$ for deviating to support the first-period outcome $(y^\#, y^\#)$ and attain the value

$$\tilde{v} = (1 - \delta)r(y^\#, y^\#) + \delta\, v^R \geq (1 - \delta)r(y^\#, B(y^\#)) + \delta\, v^*. \quad (26)$$

Abreu (1986) proposed to set $v^* = \tilde{v}$. That is, the continuation value caused by deviating from the first-period action equals the original value. This 'stick and carrot' strategy attains a value worse than repetition of Nash by promising a continuation value that is better.

A strategy that attains $\tilde{v}$ is

$$v_1 = \tilde{v}$$

$$\sigma_1(v) = \begin{cases} y^R & \text{if } v = v^R; \\ y^\# & \text{otherwise;} \end{cases} \quad (27)$$

$$\sigma_2(v, x, y) = \begin{cases} v^R & \text{if } (x, y) = (\sigma_1(v), \sigma_1(v)); \\ \tilde{v} & \text{otherwise.} \end{cases}$$

The consequence of deviating from the bad prescribed first-period government action $y^\#$ is to restart the equilibrium.

DEFINITION: A recursive SPE $(\sigma, v_1)$ is *self-enforcing* if in (27)

$$\sigma_2(v, \sigma_1(v), \eta) = v_1 \quad \forall \quad \eta \neq \sigma_1(v).$$

DEFINITION: A recursive SPE $(\sigma, v_1)$ is *self-rewarding* if in (27),

$$\sigma_2(v, \sigma_1(v), \sigma_1(v)) = v.$$

*The worst SPE*

APS (1990) showed how to find the entire set of equilibrium values $V$. In the current setting, their ideas imply:

1. The set of equilibrium values $V$ attainable by the government is a compact subset $[\underline{v}, \bar{v}]$ of $[r(y^*, y^*), 0]$.

2. The worst equilibrium value can be computed from a simple programming problem.

3. Given the worst equilibrium value, the best equilibrium value can be computed from a programming problem.

4. Given a $v \in [\underline{v}, \bar{v}]$, it is easy to construct an equilibrium that attains it.

Here is how these ideas apply.

PROPOSITION: The worst SPE is self-enforcing.

Let $\underline{v}$ be the minimum value associated with a SPE with value $\bar{v}$ the maximum value and $V = [\underline{v}, \bar{v}]$. Evidently, $\underline{v}$ satisfies

$$\underline{v} = \min_{y \in Y, v_1 \in V} \left[ (1 - \delta) r(y, y) + \delta v_1 \right]$$

subject to

$$(1 - \delta) r(y, y) + \delta v_1 \geq (1 - \delta) r(y, B(y)) + \delta \underline{v}. \tag{28}$$

In (28), we use the worst SPE as the continuation value in the event of a deviation. The minimum will be attained when the constraint is binding, which implies that $\underline{v} = r(y, B(y))$, for some government action $y$. Thus, the problem of finding the worst SPE reduces to solving

$$\underline{v} = \min_{y \in Y} r(y, B(y));$$

then computing $v_1$ from $(1 - \delta) r(y^*, y^*) + \delta v_1 = \underline{v}$ where $y^* = \arg \min r(y, B(y))$; and finally checking that $v_1$ is itself a value associated with a SPE. To check this condition, we need to know $\bar{v}$. Before we show how to check this, we note that this construction shows the following:

PROPOSITION: The best SPE is self-rewarding.

After we have computed a candidate for the worst SPE value $\underline{v}$, we can compute a candidate for the *best* value $\bar{v}$ by solving the programming problem

$$\bar{v} = \max_{y \in Y} r(y, y)$$

$$\text{s.t.} \quad r(y, y) \geq (1 - \delta)r(y, B(y)) + \delta\underline{v}.$$

Here we are assuming that $\bar{v}$ is the maximizing continuation value available to reward adherence to the policy, so that $\bar{v} = (1 - \delta)r(y, y) + \delta\bar{v}$. Let $y^b$ be the maximizing value of $y$. Once we have computed $\bar{v}$, we can check that the continuation value $v_1$ for supporting the worst value is within our candidate set $[\underline{v}, \bar{v}]$. If it is, we have succeeded in constructing $V$.

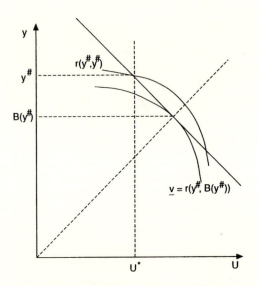

**Figure 4.1.** Calculation of the worst subgame equilibrium value $\underline{v}$.

*Multiplicity*

Two layers of multiplicity inhabit this theory. First, there is a continuum of equilibrium values. Second, many outcome paths have the same value. To illustrate how multiple outcome paths $(y, y)$ can attain the same equilibrium value, we construct several equilibria that attain the worst equilibrium value.

*Attaining the worst, method 1.*

Many SPE's attain the worst value $\underline{v}$. To compute one such SPE strategy, we can use the following recursive procedure:

(i) Set the first-period promised value $v_1 = \underline{v} = r(y^{\#}, B(y^{\#}))$. See Figure 4.1. The highest feasible inflation rate is $y^{\#}$. The worst one-period value that is consistent with rational expectations is $r(y^{\#}, y^{\#})$. Given expectations $x = y^{\#}$, the government is tempted toward $B(y^{\#}) < y^{\#}$, which yields one-period utility to the government of $r(y^{\#}, B(y^{\#}))$.

Then use $\underline{v}$ as continuation value in the event of a deviation, and construct an increasing sequence of continuation values to reward adherence, as follows.

(ii) Solve $\underline{v} = (1 - \delta)r(y^{\#}, y^{\#}) + \delta v_2$ for continuation value $v_2$.

(iii) For $j = 2, 3, \cdots$, continue solving $v_j = (1 - \delta)r(y^{\#}, y^{\#}) + \delta v_{j+1}$ for the continuation values $v_{j+1}$ so long as $v_{j+1} \leq \bar{v}$. If $v_{j+1}$ threatens to violate this constraint at step $j = \bar{j}$, then go to step (iv).

(iv) Use $\bar{v}$ as the continuation value, and solve $v_j = (1 - \delta)r(\tilde{y}, \tilde{y}) + \delta \bar{v}$ for the prescription $\tilde{y}$ to be followed if promised value $v_j$ is encountered.

(v) Set $v_{j+s} = \bar{v}$ for $s \geq 1$.

*Attaining the worst, method 2.*

To construct another equilibrium supporting the worst SPE value, follow steps (i) and (ii) above, and follow step (iii) also, except that we continue solving $v_j = (1 - \delta)r(y^{\#}, y^{\#}) + \delta v_{j+1}$ for the continuation values $v_{j+1}$ only so long as $v_{j+1} < v^N$. As soon as $v_{j+1} = v^{**} > v^N$, we use $v^{**}$ as both the promised value and the continuation value there after. Whenever $v^{**} = r(y^{**}, y^{**})$ is the promised value, $\sigma_1(v^{**}) = y^{**}$.

*Attaining the worst, method 3.*

Here is another subgame perfect equilibrium that supports $\underline{v}$. Proceed as in step (i) to find continuation value $v_2$. Now set all the subsequent values and continuation values to $v_2$, with associated first-period outcome $\tilde{y}$ which solves $v_2 = r(\tilde{y}, \tilde{y})$. It can be checked that the incentive constraint is satisfied with $\underline{v}$ the continuation value in the event of a deviation.

*Numerical examples*

Set $[\delta \quad \theta \quad U^* \quad y^{\#}] = [.95 \quad 1.2500 \quad 5.5000 \quad 10.0000]$. Compute $[x^N \quad x^R] = [6.8750 \quad 0]$, $[v^R \quad v^N \quad \underline{v} \quad v_{\text{abreu}}] = [-15.1250 \quad -38.7578 \quad -63.2195 \quad -17.6250]$. We attain the worst subgame perfect equilibrium value $\underline{v}$ with any of the sequences of time-$t$ (promised value, action) pairs depicted in Figures 4.2, 4.3, or 4.4. These figures illustrate the preceding three types of equilibria supporting the worst equilibrium value $\underline{v}$.

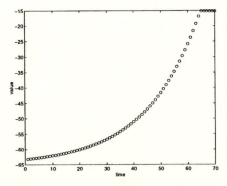

**Figure 4.2a.** Continuation values (on ordinate axis) of a SPE that attains $\underline{v}$.

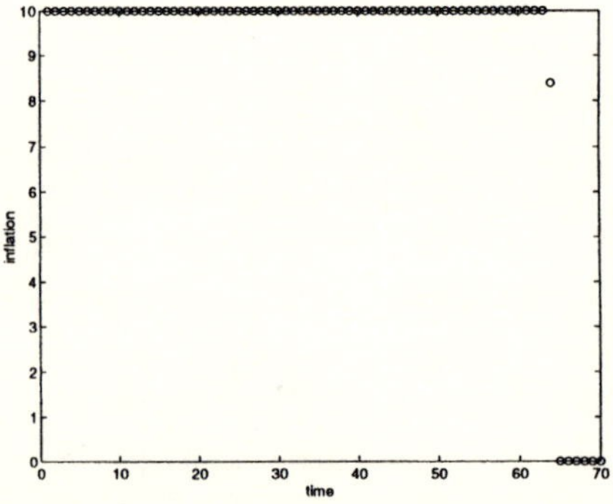

**Figure 4.2b.** Inflation values associated with those continuation values.

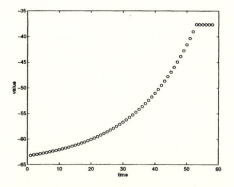

**Figure 4.3a.** Continuation values (on ordinate axis) of a SPE that attains $\underline{v}$.

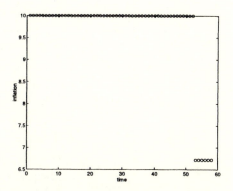

**Figure 4.3b.** Inflation values associated with those continuation values.

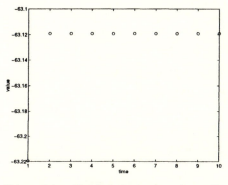

**Figure 4.4a.** Continuation values (on ordinate axis) of a SPE that attains $\underline{v}$.

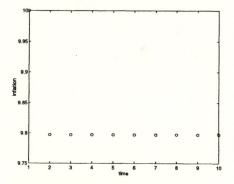

**Figure 4.4b.** Inflation values associated with those continuation values.

The cutoff value of $\delta$ below which reversion to Nash fails to support Ramsey forever is .2807. For $\delta = .2$, Abreu's stick and carrot equilibrium that calls for the outcome $(y^{\#}, y^{\#})$ for one period to be followed by $(0,0)$ forever yields value $v_{\text{Abreu}} = -55.125$. For $\delta = .2$, the simple Abreu stick-and-carrot strategy supports repetition of Ramsey even though infinite reversion to Nash fails to do so.

## Interpretations

The literature on credible plans bears mixed prospects for better than Nash outcomes and for our triumph of natural-rate theory story. The theory has many equilibria, some better and others worse than Kydland and Prescott's. The multitude of outcomes mutes the model empirically and undermines the intention of early researchers to use the rational expectations hypothesis to eliminate parameters describing expectations.

In his 1979 review of an OECD report on macroeconomic policies edited by Paul McCracken (1977), Lucas protested the report's recommendation that 'Governments should try to promote good expectations' as though expectations were an extra set of policy instruments. That recommendation misinterpreted what rational expectations meant for macroeconomics in 1979. Most rational expectations macroeconomic models then assumed exogenous government policies and made expectations functions of government policies. Cross-equation restrictions linked expectations to laws of motion for government instruments and other exogenous variables.[9]

The literature on credible government policy turns systems of expectations into free parameters that influence outcomes but that cannot necessarily be chosen by the government or anybody else inside the model. The government complies with equilibrium expectations about its behavior. These models isolate systems of expectations in which governments have reputations that they want to sustain. They do not model how a reputation is acquired or altered. The government's strategy plays two roles: as a decision rule, and as a description of the private sector's expectations, which restrain the government. It is impossible to disentangle them within an equilibrium.

---

[9] For some environments, this statement has to qualified in light of the possibility that equilibria are indexed by sunspots. See Woodford (1990) for references to that literature, and for a theory of how adaptive agents might settle upon such an equilibrium.

The authors of the McCracken report believed in multiplicity and manipulation while Lucas doubted both. The literature on credible plans supports multiplicity but not manipulation.

*Remedies*

Reputation alone is a weak foundation for anti-inflation policy. This fact has inspired proposals to change the game to assure a good outcome. Kenneth Rogoff (1985) proposed altering the government's preferences by delegating conduct of inflation policy to someone who doesn't care about unemployment.[10] Assigning inflation policy to someone who is unaware even of a temporary trade-off between inflation and unemployment would be equally effective. Having sets of central bankers indexed by different inflation–unemployment preferences[11] can also improve the outcome.[12]

I now explore a different route to better outcomes beginning with the notion that the multiplicity of equilibria within models of credible policy stems from the rationality assigned to all participants in the system. To eradicate multiplicity, I retreat from perfection and move to models in which some people have a more limited understanding of the economy. These models are closer to what Lucas imagined when he criticized the McCracken report.

[10] Alan Blinder (1998) suggested a related idea: that the monetary authority be someone who knows the natural rate of unemployment each period, and who never wants unemployment to differ from it.
[11] Some of the potential policy makers are like Rogoff's conservative and others are like the authority in Kydland and Prescott's original model.
[12] See Barro and Gordon (1983) and Ball (1995).

# 5
## Adaptive Expectations (1950's)

They cannot look out far.
They cannot look in deep.
But when was that ever a bar
To any watch they keep?

Robert Frost

### Adaptive expectations

This chapter describes the Cagan-Friedman adaptive expectations hypothesis, how Phelps used it to formulate the natural-rate hypothesis, and its role in the initial econometric tests of the natural-rate hypothesis. Results in this early literature form building blocks for my later work with a modern form of adaptation.

#### The original Phelps problem

Edmund Phelps (1967) formulated a control problem for a natural-rate model. He dropped rationality for the public, but not for the government,[1] and assigned the public a particular mechanical forecasting rule known to the government.[2]

The economy repeats forever, and the government evaluates outcome sequences according to (18). When $\delta = 1$, we interpret (18) in the usual limit of means (Cesaro sum) sense:

---

[1]  Note the reversal of Lucas's (1976) recommendation.
[2]  Stanley Fischer (1986) and Peter Ireland (1997) describe how imputing to the government such a model of the public's expectations promotes behavior that resembles a concern for reputation.

$\liminf_{T\to\infty} T^{-1}\sum_{t=1}^{T} r(x_t, y_t)$. The public uses the adaptive expectations scheme of Milton Friedman and Philip Cagan:

$$x_t - x_{t-1} = (1 - \lambda)(y_{t-1} - x_{t-1}), \tag{29}$$

where $\lambda \in (0,1)$. Notice how (29) is a constant coefficient or constant gain version of the least squares learning algorithm (6), where $(1 - \lambda)$ takes the role of $t^{-1}$ in (6). Equation (29) can be represented in the form

$$x_t = (1 - \lambda)\sum_{i=1}^{\infty} \lambda^{i-1} y_{t-i}. \tag{30}$$

Equation (30) possesses what Cho and Matsui (1995) call an induction property: if the government keeps repeating a constant $y_t = \bar{y}$ policy, eventually the public comes nearly to set $x = \bar{y}$. Solow and Tobin imposed this property in testing the natural unemployment rate hypothesis.

Let $p(U_t, y_t) = -.5(U_t^2 + y_t^2)$. The government's problem is to maximize

$$V^g(U, y) = (1 - \delta)\sum_{t=1}^{\infty} \delta^{t-1} p(U_t, y_t), \quad \delta \in (0,1) \tag{31}$$

(i.e., (18)) by choice of a rule for $y_t$, subject to (29) and the Phillips curve (3) $U_t = U^* - \theta(y_t - x_t)$, given initial conditions for $(y_{-1}, x_{-1})$. The state for the government's control problem is $[1 \quad y_{t-1} \quad x_{t-1}]'$. The solution of the government's problem takes the form $y_t = f_1 + f_2[\lambda x_{t-1} + (1 - \lambda)y_{t-1}] = f_1 + f_2 x_t$, with $f_1 \neq 0, f_2 \neq 1$, inequalities that reflect that the public does not use an optimal forecasting rule in setting $x_t$.[3]

---

[3] Note that $f_1 = 0, f_2 = 1$ implies that $y_t = x_t$ for all histories of $x_t$ and $y_t$. Imposing the induction property sets $y_t \approx x_t$ only for particular histories of $y_t$, and what may be very untypical ones at that. This is the start of Lucas's (1972) and Sargent's (1971) criticisms of the Solow-Tobin way of testing the natural-rate hypothesis. Despite criticizing Tobin and Solow's identification scheme in 1972, Lucas (1980) used it. Charles Whiteman (1983) criticized Lucas's 1980 procedure.

Our interest in this control problem stems from the following result:

PROPOSITION ($\delta = 1$ EVENTUALLY SUSTAINS RAMSEY): In the absence of discounting, the government drives $y_t$ to $0$, the Ramsey outcome.

When $\delta = 1$, $\lambda$ governs the speed of convergence to the Ramsey outcome. When $\delta < 1$, the limit point of $y_t$ depends on a comparison of $\lambda$ with $\delta$. For $\lambda < \delta$ and $\delta$ close to 1, the government's policy eventually approximates the Ramsey outcome. The public's expectations are wrong along the transition path, but are correct in the steady state, by virtue of the induction property.

For parameter values $\theta = 1, U^* = 5$, Tables 1a and 1b summarize optimal disinflation paths for $\delta = .96$ (Table 1a) and $\delta = 1$ (Table 1b) for the two values $\lambda = .7, .9$. We started the government's control problem from the late 1970's initial conditions $x_{-1} = y_{-1} = 12$. These initial conditions imply that $U = U^* = 5$. Notice how for each of the four parameter settings, the government engineers a major recession and immediately brings inflation down more than half way toward its eventual limiting value. This happens even for the long lag specification $\lambda = .9$. Notice also how in the discounted ($\delta = .96$) case, the government accepts a longer but milder recession when $\lambda = .9$ than when $\lambda = .7$.

Some dynamics in these tables resurfaces in later chapters in more sophisticated adaptive schemes that alter the assumption that $\lambda$ is a free parameter. The self-confirming and forecast misspecification types of equilibria, presented in Chapter 7, transform $\lambda$ from a free parameter to an equilibrium outcome. Nevertheless, the beneficial role of the induction hypothesis will survive.

**Table 1a.**
Paths of unemployment and inflation starting from
$y_{-1} = 12$, $x_{-1} = 12$ with $\delta = .96$ and $\lambda = .7$ and $.9$.

| lags | $\lambda = .7$ | | $\lambda = .9$ | |
|---|---|---|---|---|
| | U | y | U | y |
| 1 | 12.6 | 4.4 | 11.9 | 5.1 |
| 5 | 8.1 | 2.2 | 10.2 | 4.3 |
| 20 | 5.1 | .7 | 6.9 | 2.5 |
| 50 | 5.0 | .6 | 5.2 | 1.6 |

**Table 1b.**
Paths of unemployment and inflation starting from
$y_{-1} = 12$, $x_{-1} = 12$ with $\delta = 1$ and $\lambda = .7$ and $.9$.

| lags | $\lambda = .7$ | | $\lambda = .9$ | |
|---|---|---|---|---|
| | U | y | U | y |
| 1 | 13.2 | 3.8 | 13.4 | 3.6 |
| 5 | 8.3 | 1.5 | 11.3 | 2.7 |
| 20 | 5.1 | 0.1 | 7.1 | 0.9 |
| 50 | 5.0 | 0.0 | 5.2 | 0.1 |

## Phelps problem: general version

For Phelps's control problem, the reduced form of the Phillips curve matters, not the underlying structure identifying $x_t$. It is useful to state a more general version of the Phelps problem that assumes that the government's model is a reduced form distributed lag Phillips curve. Define the vectors $X_{Ut-1} = [U_{t-1} \quad \cdots \quad U_{t-m_U}]'$, $X_{yt-1} = [y_{t-1} \quad \cdots \quad y_{t-m_y}]'$, $X_t = [X'_{Ut} \quad X'_{yt} \quad 1]'$. Notice that $X_{Ut-1}$ and $X_{yt-1}$, and therefore $X_{t-1}$ also, are defined to include information dated $t-1$ and earlier; $X_{t-1}$ is the state vector for the general Phelps problem. I specify alternative reduced form (distributed lag) Phillips curves whose regressors are $X_{Ct} = [y_t \quad X'_{t-1}]'$ and $X_{Kt} = [U_t \quad X'_{t-1}]'$, respectively. The subscripts C and K stand for Classical and Keynesian. For convenience, Table 2 records various objects that occur frequently in the Phelps problem. These same objects reappear in the definitions of self-confirming

equilibria and in the 1990's adaptive models of Chapters 8 and
9.

**Table 2**

Objects in the Phelps problem

| Object | Meaning |
|---|---|
| $X_{Ut}$ | $[U_{t-1}, \ldots, U_{t-m_u}]'$ |
| $X_{yt}$ | $[y_{t-1}, \ldots, y_{t-m_y}]'$ |
| $X_t$ | $[X'_{Ut}, X'_{yt}, 1]'$ |
| $X_{Ct}$ | $[y_t \ X'_{t-1}]'$ |
| $X_{Kt}$ | $[U_t \ X'_{t-1}]'$ |
| Class. Phillips curve | $U_t = [\gamma_1 \ \gamma'_{-1}]' X_{Ct} + \varepsilon_{Ct}$ |
| Keynes Phillips curve | $y_t = [\beta_1 \ \beta - 1']' X_{Kt} + \varepsilon_{Kt}$ |
| $\gamma$ | coeffnts (classical) |
| $\beta$ | coeffnts (Keynesian) |
| $h(\gamma)$ | coeffnts of govt rule |

We define the Phelps problem in terms of the classical Phillips
curve:

$$U_t = \gamma' X_{Ct} + \varepsilon_{Ct}, \qquad (32a)$$

or

$$U_t = [\gamma_1 \ \gamma'_{-1}] \begin{bmatrix} y_t \\ X_{t-1} \end{bmatrix} + \varepsilon_{Ct} \qquad (32b)$$

where $\varepsilon_{Ct}$ is perceived to be random noise. The government
ranks outcome paths according to the mathematical expectation
of (31). The government believes that it sets $y_t$, apart from a
random term, so that

$$y_t = \hat{y}_t + v_{2t}, \qquad (33)$$

where $v_{2t}$ is a white noise that is beyond the government's
control and is orthogonal to information dated $t-1$ and earlier;
$\hat{y}_t$ can be set by the government as a function of information
known at $t-1$.

DEFINITION: The *Phelps problem* is to choose a control law $\hat{y}_t = hX_{t-1}$ to maximize the expected value of (31) subject to (32) and
(33).

The Phelps problem induces a mapping from the government's beliefs $\gamma$ to the government's decision rule for setting inflation $h$:

$$h = h(\gamma). \tag{34}$$

The control problem in the previous section is a special case of the Phelps problem that imposed the restrictions on $\gamma$ in (32) that come from substituting the adaptive expectations hypothesis (29) into (3). Notice that once that substitution has been made, the state variable $x_t$ remains hidden for the rest of the analysis.

In the more general Phelps problem, the induction hypothesis would make the weights on current and lagged $y$'s in (32) sum to zero. We can express the induction hypothesis in terms of its implications for the inverse relationship obtained by solving (32) for $y_t$:

$$y_t = \beta' X_{Kt} + \varepsilon_{Kt}, \tag{35a}$$

or

$$y_t = [\beta_1 \quad \beta'_{-1}] \begin{bmatrix} U_t \\ X_{t-1} \end{bmatrix} + \varepsilon_{Kt} \tag{35b}$$

where $\varepsilon_{Kt}$ is another random disturbance. We can compute $\gamma$ from $\beta$ (and vice versa) using the relations

$$\gamma_1 = \beta_1^{-1}, \quad \gamma_{-1} = -\beta_{-1}/\beta_1. \tag{36}$$

When the Phillips curve is expressed as (35), the induction hypothesis implies that the sum of weights on lagged $y$'s equals unity. This brings us to Solow's and Tobin's early proposal for testing the natural-rate hypothesis.

### Testing the natural-rate hypothesis

Solow (1968) and Tobin (1968) exploited the induction hypothesis. They substituted (30) into an inverted version of the Phillips curve (3) to get

$$y_t = (1 - \lambda) \sum_{i=1}^{\infty} \lambda^{i-1} y_{t-i} + \theta^{-1}(U^* - U_t). \tag{37}$$

They proposed to test the natural-rate hypothesis by running a regression of the form

$$y_t = b_0 + b_1(1 - \lambda) \sum_{i=1}^{\infty} \lambda^{i-1} y_{t-i} + b_2 U_t + \varepsilon_t, \qquad (38)$$

where $\varepsilon_t$ is a least squares residual. They interpreted a finding that $b_1 < 1$ as indicating a long-run trade-off between inflation and unemployment of slope $b_1 - 1$. An alternative was to fit a less restricted distributed lag

$$y_t = \tilde{\beta}_0 + \tilde{\beta}_1(L)y_{t-1} + \tilde{\beta}_2(L)U_t + \varepsilon_{Kt}, \qquad (39)$$

where $\tilde{\beta}_1(L) = \sum_{j=1}^{m_y} \tilde{\beta}_{1,j}L^j$, $\tilde{\beta}_2(L) = \sum_{j=0}^{m_U} \tilde{\beta}_{2,j}L^j$, and $L$ is the lag operator. In this version, the natural-rate hypothesis is taken to be $\tilde{\beta}_1(1) = 1$. Early implementations of the tests found that $b_1 < 1$ (or $\tilde{\beta}_1(1) < 1$) and so rejected the natural-rate hypothesis in favor of a long-run trade-off between inflation and unemployment.[4] Later implementations of the same tests failed to reject the natural-rate hypothesis. According to an argument of Sargent (1971) and King and Watson (1994), that pattern is consistent with the tendency of inflation to have exhibited a unit root after the 1960's but not before.[5]

---

[4] Lucas (1972) and Sargent (1971) argued that those rejections did not bear on the adequacy of the natural-rate hypothesis. Tobin and Solow deduced the restriction $b_1 = 1$ in effect by using the induction hypothesis to achieve econometric identification of expected inflation in (38). Lucas and Sargent described specific stationary stochastic processes for which the hypothesis that the $w_i$'s add up to one in $x_t = \sum_{i=1}^{\infty} w_i y_{t-i}$ contradicted the hypothesis of rational expectations. They showed how rational expectations imposed restrictions across the $w_i$'s and the stochastic process governing the inflation process in the sample period. The induction hypothesis imposes a restriction on $\sum_i w_i$ from a particular experiment (i.e., a permanent and fixed inflation) that could be very unlikely for many stochastic processes. King and Watson (1994) have revisited this issue, and emphasized that the unit-sum restriction is compatible with rational expectations where $y_t$ has a unit root.

[5] See King and Watson (1994).

*Disappearance of beliefs as state variable*

The private sector's expectations about inflation, $x_t$, disappear from the Phelps problem. They are replaced by technical conditions on the zero-frequency characteristics of the distributed lag of $y_t$ appearing on the right side of (38) or (39). The ideas of adaptation and induction are also de-emphasized, as is the natural-rate hypothesis itself. From the viewpoint of Phelps's control problem, it is incidental whether the natural-rate hypothesis holds. The Phelps problem imparts interesting dynamics to the inflation-unemployment choice, whether or not $b_1 = 1$ in (38).

*Subversion of Phelps's model*

This observation recalls a reaction that accompanied the increasing tendency of tests administered during the 1970's to confirm the natural-rate hypothesis in U.S. data. That reaction was based on thinking about the Phelps problem in the context of large $\lambda$'s in (30) or long mean lags on lagged $y$'s in (35). In the Phelps problem under (30), for a fixed $\delta < 1$, it is always possible to find a $\lambda$ close enough to 1 so that high inflationary expectations $x_{t-1}$ will make a government want to avoid the Ramsey outcome.[6] In the late 1970's, models with long expectations adjustment lags were used to recommend against reducing inflation.[7] Large sacrifice ratios – estimated amounts of foregone GDP required to bring inflation down one percentage point – circulated widely in the U.S. in the late 1970's. Despite its encouraging implications in terms of sustaining the Ramsey

---

[6] But remember the calculations in Table 1. To push the model away from a recommendation for taking a large recession to earn a quick reduction of a high inflation, one would have to put even longer lags into inflation expectations.

[7] By stressing the cross-equation restrictions embedded in rational expectations versions of the natural-rate hypothesis, the analyses of Lucas (1972) and Sargent (1971) asserted that historical estimates of $\lambda$ were silent about an optimal speed of disinflation. See Sargent (1986) for an extended treatment of this issue in the context of stabilizations of big inflations.

outcome under the induction hypothesis, Phelps's control problem carries a tattered past. It fortified those in the 1970's who advocated learning to live with high inflation because of the unacceptably high costs in unemployment from disinflating.

Nevertheless, the Phelps problem illustrates how activating the induction hypothesis can eventually lead to better outcomes. In the form that Phelps, Tobin, and Solow used, the induction hypothesis retreats from rational expectations.[8]

In Chapters 7 and 8, I impute to the government and the public more symmetry in their understandings and procedures to form models that apply up-dating schemes like (29) to functions rather than to numbers.

The next chapter takes a detour to introduce a type of approximate equilibrium under adaptive expectations. In this equilibrium, $\lambda$ in (30) disappears as a parameter and becomes an equilibrium outcome. In the subsequent chapter, I describe a 1970's rational expectations model. These two models contain important elements of the dynamics of our *circa* 1990's adaptive expectations models.

---

[8] But Marianne Baxter (1985), Stanley Fischer (1986), and Peter Ireland (1997) have noted that the adaptive expectations model (29) responds much like rational expectations models where policy makers are drawn from a probability distribution over types of preferences.

# 6
## *Optimal Misspecified Beliefs*

### *Equilibrium with mistakes*

This chapter describes three key conceptual issues:

1. How to formulate equilibria where agents have a common misspecified least squares forecasting model.

2. How expectations can contribute independent dynamics within equilibria.

3. How within such equilibria the classic adaptive expectations scheme can use second moments to approximate a first moment.

These issues recur throughout this essay. To expose them, I temporarily set aside the Phillips curve example, and formulate the issues in terms of Bray's (1982) simple model of the price of a single good. This model is a work horse for studying bounded rationality. I alter Bray's model to illustrate an equilibrium concept that merges aspects of rational and adaptive expectations in a new way. Later I apply this equilibrium concept to the Phillips curve model.

I focus on market equilibrium with optimal but misspecified forecasts. Optimal means that the free parameters of the forecasting scheme are chosen by maximum likelihood or generalized least squares. Misspecified means that the forecasting model is wrong either in functional form or in using too small an information set. The true model depends on how market participants' model is misspecified.

## An experiment in Bray's lab

I follow Bray (1982) and assume that

$$p_t = a + bp_{t+1}^e + u_t \qquad (40)$$

where $u_t$ is i.i.d., with mean zero and variance $\sigma_u^2$; $a > 0, b \in (0,1)$; $p_t$ is the market price of a good; and $p_{t+1}^e$ is the market's expectation of the price. The rational expectations equilibrium has $p_{t+1}^e = \frac{a}{1-b}$, and $p_t = \frac{a}{1-b} + u_t$.

In place of rational expectations, Bray posited that $p_{t+1}^e$ is the empirical average of past prices, which can be represented recursively as $p_{t+1}^e = p_t^e + t^{-1}(p_{t-1} - p_t^e)$. With these expectations, Bray showed that when $0 < b < 1$, $p_{t+1}^e$ converges almost surely to the rational expectation $\frac{a}{1-b}$. During a transition to rational expectations, while learning continues, the state variable $p_t^e$ contributes dynamics and makes the price serially correlated. But Bray showed that these dynamics are transitory.[1] At the rational expectations equilibrium, $p_t$ is a constant plus a serially uncorrelated shock.

To let expectations impart persistent serial correlation to the price, I depart from Bray and assume that the market has adaptive expectations of the form

$$p_{t+1}^e = Cp_t + (1 - C)p_t^e, \qquad (41)$$

where $|C| < 1$. Notice how, in effect, Bray assumed a version of (41) in which $\frac{1}{t}$ replaces $C$, which makes $p_{t+1}^e$ become a sample average of past $p$'s. In contrast, the algorithm with a fixed $C$ as in (41) is known as a fixed gain algorithm. Fixing $C$ has the effect of discounting past observations, relative to Bray's scheme. If $C \in (0,1)$, (41) is a version of adaptive expectations, past observations discounted at a rate $C - 1$. Discounting past observations arrests convergence to rational expectations

---

[1] See Sargent (1993, Chapter 5) for a graph of these transient dynamics.

and prevents the state variable $p_{t+1}^e$ from converging to a constant. Instead, it can converge to a serially correlated stationary stochastic process.

Equation (41) would be the linear least squares forecast if the price were to follow the process

$$p_t = p_{t-1} + \epsilon_t - (1 - C)\epsilon_{t-1}, \tag{42}$$

where $\epsilon_t$ is a serially uncorrelated process that equals the one-step ahead error in forecasting $p_t$ linearly from its own past. With this specification the market sees the price as composed of purely permanent and transitory components.[2]

I want to formulate a mapping whose fixed point delivers a reasonable concept of equilibrium under misspecification. I begin by describing how the price actually moves when the market's beliefs are (41). Equation (41) can be rearranged to be

$$p_{t+1}^e = \frac{C}{1 - (1 - C)L} p_t \tag{43}$$

where $C \in (0, 1)$. Substituting (43) into (40) shows that when people in the market believe that the price should be forecast according to (43), their actions make the actual law of motion for price become

$$p_t = \frac{a}{(1 - b)} + \frac{1}{(1 - bC)} \left[ \frac{1 - (1 - C)L}{1 - \frac{1 - C}{1 - bC}L} \right] u_t, \tag{44a}$$

or

$$p_t = \nu + f(L)u_t \tag{44b}$$

where $\nu, f(L)$ are defined to match the last two equations. The first and second moments of $p_t$ are described by the stationary mean $\nu$ and the spectrum

$$F(\omega) = f(\exp(i\omega))f(\exp(-i\omega))\sigma_u^2, \quad \omega \in [-\pi, \pi].$$

---

[2] See Muth (1960).

Notice that $F(\omega)$ depends on $C$, through $f$.

When $C$ is a small positive number, the perceived law of motion (42) differs from the actual one (44a) in interesting ways. Equation (44b) has a constant, plus a mixed moving average, autoregressive piece. The perceived law has to emulate a constant through its unit root.

*Misspecification*

To motivate a restriction on $C$, note two important facts about (44): (a) given that the price obeys (44), the linear least squares one-step forecasting rule, conditioned on the infinite history of $p_t$, is not a geometric distributed lag like (41). And (b), even if we were to restrict the expectations rule to take the form (41), the best forecasting rule of this class would make $C$ solve a forecast error minimization problem and thereby make $C$ an outcome, not a parameter. A rational expectations equilibrium repairs both of these dimensions. I soften the equilibrium concept by leaving feature (a) untouched, while fixing dimension (b).

Think of putting a single individual into this market and of constraining him to use a rule of the form (41). Suppose that everyone else, called the market or the representative agent, uses $C$, making the equilibrium price obey (44).[3] We assume that the single individual chooses a $c$ to yield the best fitting model of the form:[4]

$$p_t = \frac{1 - (1 - c)L}{1 - L}\epsilon_t \qquad (45a)$$

[3] This 'big C, little c' formalism parallels constructions of Stokey (1989) and many others, but here the decision rule is a forecast function. Evans and Honkapohja (1993) formulate and compute a closely related approximate equilibrium under a constant gain learning rule. Their $\delta$ plays the role of our $c$. Their economic model is nonlinear and has multiple rational expectations equilibria. They use computer simulations to approximate an equilibrium setting of a gain parameter. Marcet and Nicolini (1997) also use computer simulations to approximate equilibria under a constant gain algorithm.

[4] I should defend dividing through by (1-L). Two methods in the literature are to divide through by $(1 - \rho L)$, where $\rho$ is made to approach 1 from below; or to set initial conditions that initialize the $\{\epsilon_t\}$ process to be zero before some date.

or

$$p_t = g(L)\epsilon_t. \qquad (45b)$$

The individual uses a forecasting rule parameterized by $c$, and chooses $c$ to minimize the one-step ahead forecasting error.[5]

The market sets $C$, and the individual sets $c$, given $C$. Proceeding in the spirit (but not the letter) of Lucas and Prescott (1971) and Brock (1972), I propose the following:

DEFINITION: Given $C$ and the consequent stochastic process for the price (44), an individual's best forecast parameter $c = B(C)$ is the nonlinear least squares estimator of $c$ in (45a), where the data are generated by (44).

Given $(a, b, \sigma_u^2)$, the nonlinear least squares problem induces a mapping $c = B(C)$. To complete our equilibrium concept, we shall use this best-estimate map like a best-response map. Given $C$, $c$ solves the following minimum variance problem:

$$\hat{c} = B(C) = \text{argmin}_c \left\{ E \left[ g(L;c)^{-1} \left( \nu + f(L;C)u_t \right) \right]^2 \right\}, \qquad (46)$$

where the expectation is taken with respect to the distribution of the $u_t$'s. I deduced this expression for $E\epsilon_t^2$ by inverting (45b) to write $\epsilon_t = g(L)^{-1}p_t$, then using (44b) for $p_t$. Let the minimized value of the criterion on the right side of (46) be denoted $\bar{\sigma}_\epsilon^2$. This is the *actual* variance of one step ahead forecast errors associated with using the misspecified model (45).[6]

---

[5] To facilitate the minimization that defines $B(C)$ using the frequency domain calculations in the footnote below, I approximated $g(L)$ in (45) by $\frac{1-(1-c)L}{1-\rho L}$ where $\rho < 1$ and set $\rho$ close to 1. This approximation keeps the spectral density of the approximating model well defined.

[6] The parameter $\sigma_\epsilon$ has been concentrated out in this nonlinear least squares problem, and can be determined as the optimized value of (46). In calculating, we follow Sims (1993) and Hansen and Sargent (1993) by working in the frequency domain. The free parameters in (45) are $c, \sigma_\epsilon^2$. The process has mean 0 and spectrum $G(\omega) = g(\exp(i\omega))g(\exp(-i\omega))\sigma_\epsilon^2$. Notice that $G(\omega)$ depends on $c$, through $g(\omega)$. Following Hansen and Sargent (1993), the best approximating

For a given $C$, the right side of (46) is an approximation problem like the ones of Sims (1971) and White (1982, 1994), who in various contexts studied the behavior of maximum likelihood estimators of misspecified models. Their formulations apply here because the agents inside our model behave like econometricians with misspecified models.

We must go beyond Sims's and White's formulations for the following reason. In their formulations, the true model is fixed from outside and does not depend on estimates of the approximating model; but in our setting, it will. This can be seen directly from (44), where the expectations parameter $C$ plays an important role. This equilibrium concept imposes two features: (1) given the stochastic process for the price, an individual market participant's expectation parameter $c$ must satisfy (46); and (2) the representative agent must be representative, requiring $C = B(C)$. These features are captured in:

DEFINITION: An equilibrium under forecast misspecification is a fixed point of $B$.

Kalai and Lehrer (1993) applied a theorem of Blackwell and Dubins (1962) to establish general conditions under which forecasts eventually must merge with rational expectations. The present model shuts off the Blackwell-Dubins mechanism at the outset because the agents' model is wrong.[7] In an equilibrium

$c, \sigma_\epsilon^2$ can be computed by minimizing with respect to $c, \sigma_\epsilon^2$ the expression

$$A(c, \sigma_\epsilon^2) = \frac{1}{N} \sum_{j=0}^{N-1} \left\{ \log G(\omega_j, c) + [G(\omega_j, c)^{-1} F(\omega_j)] + v^2 G(0)^{-1} \right\}, \quad (47)$$

where $\omega_j = \frac{2\pi j}{N}$, for $j = 0, \ldots, N-1$. The sum approximates $(2\pi)^{-1}$ times the integral from $-\pi$ to $\pi$ across frequencies. After we calculate the equilibrium $C$ and the associated $\sigma_\epsilon^2$, we form $\bar{\sigma}_\epsilon^2 = \exp K$, where $K$ is $A(C, \sigma_\epsilon^2)$ and $C = B(C)$. The quantity $\bar{\sigma}_\epsilon^2$ is the true prediction error variance associated with using the wrong model.

[7] The model puts zero probability on events that have positive probability under the truth, violating Blackwell-Dubins' absolute continuity condition. For

with forecast misspecification, sufficient data and appropriate statistical tests would eventually tell how forecasts could be improved. However, it could require a large data set. Information about how much data would be needed is contained in the relationship between the spectral densities of the true and forecasting models, which we now briefly study.

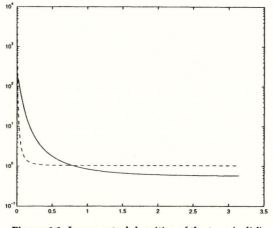

**Figure 6.1.** Log spectral densities of the true (solid) and forecasting (dotted line) models ($a = 1, b = .5, C = .081$). Angular frequency is the ordinate.

For parameters $a = 1, b = .5, \sigma_u^2 = 1$, I computed an equilibrium with misspecification to be $C = .0805, \sigma_\epsilon = 1.01579, \bar{\sigma}_\epsilon = 1.0579$. Remember that $\bar{\sigma}_\epsilon$ is the actual and $\sigma_\epsilon$ the believed one-step ahead standard error of forecast for the approximating model. For the true model, the standard error of forecast is $\frac{1}{1-b(1-C)} = 1.0208$. For these parameter values, Figure 6.1 plots the equilibrium spectral densities of the true and misspecified models. In interpreting this graph, it is important to remember that in minimizing (47), the approximating model is using the

discussions of merging results and their relevance for models of learning, see Kalai and Lehrer (1993) and Marimon (1997).

unit root to fit the mean.[8] Thus, the large gap between the spectral densities at low frequencies reflects how the approximating models fit first moment with features of second moments.[9]
The least squares problem sets the one parameter $C = B(C)$ to
achieve a compromise across frequencies.[10]

The true spectral density of the price process in Figure 6.1 has
Granger's (1968) typical spectral shape, decreasing sharply with
increases in frequency. This shape reveals substantial positive
serial correlation in the price process. Agents' beliefs that the
price is subject to permanent shocks, as reflected in (40), cause
shocks to have persistent effects on price.

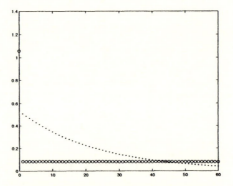

**Figure 6.2.** Impulse response function of
true (dots) and approximating (circles)
model.

---

[8] This is captured in the term $\nu^2 G(0)^{-1}$ in (46).
[9] It can be shown that using unconditional second moment properties to approximate conditional first moment properties underlies the example in section
4 of Sims (1993). Sims uses a linearly indeterministic model with a constant
mean to approximate a model with a periodic mean (i.e., a seasonal dummy).
Conceptually, the only difference between Sims's example and ours is that we
have put the spike in the true spectral density at frequency zero rather than the
seasonal frequencies that preoccupied Sims.
[10] We calculated $\bar{\sigma}_\epsilon$, the actual one-step ahead standard error of prediction from
the misspecified model, to be 1.75, whereas the true model has a corresponding
standard of prediction error of 1.02.

Figure 6.2 plots impulse response functions for the true and approximating models. The impulse response for the true model affirms the serial correlation in the price. The approximating model has a tendency to under predict short term consequences of a shock while over predicting long term ones, because the true function lies above the approximating one at first, then falls below it.

## *Lessons*

The agents in the misspecified model are boundedly rational, where rational describes their use of least squares and bounded describes their model misspecification. Christopher Sims (1980) referred to bounded rationality as a wilderness for reasons that readers of this chapter may appreciate. Under the rational expectations assumption, there is only one model in play, though there can be different information sets. Under bounded rationality there must be at least two models, the one used by the boundedly rational agents, and the true one. These mutually influence each other, because the boundedly rational agents use their model to approximate the true one; and because the true one reflects the decisions of the agents. Both differ from the rational expectations model.

Beyond introducing a suitable equilibrium concept where agents use a misspecified model, the example illustrates how equilibrium serial correlation is affected as the misspecified model adjusts to match salient features of the data. The peculiar way that the adaptive expectations model uses a unit root to mimic a constant foreshadows aspects of a version of the Phillips curve model that will help vindicate econometric policy evaluation. I now return to the business of constructing that model.

# 7
## *Self-Confirming Equilibria*

### *Two literatures*

This chapter takes up the quest for models that depart minimally from the basic Kydland-Prescott model, but that also can replicate a 1960's acceleration of inflation followed by a Volcker stabilization. I combine ideas from two literatures to build imperfect rational expectations equilibria of a kind constructed in the 1970's and 1980's in response to Lucas's Critique.[1] These models fail to generate the U.S. inflation pattern because they are too close to the basic Kydland-Prescott model. But when modified slightly in Chapter 8, they take us closer to success.

### *Directions of fit*

I draw first on a literature that verifies the persistence of the Phillips curve in post-World War II U.S. time series data. King and Watson's (1994) perspective on this literature contributes a main ingredient. King and Watson carefully documented how impulse responses depend on which direction of fit is used to identify a Phillips curve. Simplifying their perspective slightly, they catalogued different inferences about dynamic responses that flow from regressing unemployment on inflation rather than inflation on unemployment.

---

[1] I use imperfect to distinguish these models from the perfect equilibria described in Chapter 4. The equilibria in this chapter will be characterized by subtle departures from the Chapter 4 assumptions about the government's understanding of the model.

*Imperfect (1970's) rational expectations equilibria*

I consider the issues raised by King and Watson's work in the context of another literature that formulates rational expectations models as fixed points of mappings from beliefs to population limits of statistical models.[2] I define and discuss a particular kind of imperfect rational expectations equilibrium, to be called a self-confirming equilibrium to admit the presence of what might be argued is irrationality on the part of the government.[3] The government has a wrong model in the sense that it misinterprets statistical regularities. But it fits its model to match the data according to least squares. I describe two examples of this type of rational expectations model which differ in the statistical model used by the government, but only in the direction of minimization used in estimation.

The equilibrium concept of this chapter identifies potential limit points for a system with adaptive agents who recursively update estimates of a model as new data become available. In the next chapter I describe adaptive models and how they approach a self-confirming equilibrium.

# Self-confirming equilibria

*Objects in Phelps problem*

The key objects in this chapter appeared in our general statement of the Phelps problem listed in Table 2 from Chapter 5 and reproduced here. They include $\gamma$, a vector of regression coefficients in the government's Phillips curve, and $h$, the coefficients in the government's decision rule. The Phelps problem makes $h$ a function of $\gamma$. The Phelps problem takes $\gamma$ as given and delivers the mapping $h(\gamma)$.

---

[2] The tradition goes back to Muth (1961) and Lucas and Prescott (1971), and is exploited by Marcet and Sargent (1989) and Evans and Honkapohja (1995).

[3] Fudenberg and Levine (1993) use the term self-confirming equilibrium to refer to a related idea.

**Table 2**
Objects in Phelps problem

| Object | Meaning |
|---|---|
| $X_{Ut}$ | $[U_{t-1}, \ldots, U_{t-m_u}]'$ |
| $X_{yt}$ | $[y_{t-1}, \ldots, y_{t-m_y}]'$ |
| $X_t$ | $[X'_{Ut}, X'_{yt}, 1]'$ |
| $X_{Ct}$ | $[y_t \, X'_{t-1}]'$ |
| $X_{Kt}$ | $[U_t \, X'_{t-1}]'$ |
| Class. Phillips curve | $U_t = [\gamma_1 \, \gamma'_{-1}]'X_{Ct} + \varepsilon_{Ct}$ |
| Keynes Phillips curve | $y_t = [\beta_1 \, \beta{-}1']'X_{Kt} + \varepsilon_{Kt}$ |
| $\gamma$ | coeffnts (classical) |
| $\beta$ | coeffnts (Keynesian) |
| $h(\gamma)$ | coeffnts of govt rule |

### Elements of self-confirming models

Self-confirming models have these parts: (i) the government's erroneous belief about the Phillips curve; (ii) the private sector's beliefs about the evolution of inflation; (iii) an optimum problem that determines the government's setting of the inflation rate; (iv) the actual expectational Phillips curve; and (v) some orthogonality conditions making beliefs consistent with the data. Unlike Chapters 3 and 4, this equilibrium concept gives the government a model that is not structural in the econometric sense of being invariant with respect to the type of intervention that it contemplates.

I describe two models that are identical in their first four elements. They differ only in element (v), the King-Watson statistical details used to interpret the estimated Phillips curve. I adopt King and Watson's classical and Keynesian identification schemes as terms to describe $U$ on $y$ and $y$ on $U$ regressions, respectively.

### The actual Phillips curve

First, I describe the actual Phillips curve, which simply extends the one used in earlier chapters to allow for serially correlated shocks. I specify a statistical version of the natural-rate Phillips curve (3) with a geometric distributed lag in surprise inflation ($y_t - x_t = v_{2t}$) and a serially correlated disturbance.[4] Thus, assume that the underlying Phillips curve is

$$U_t = U^* - \frac{\theta}{1 - \rho_2 L} (y_t - x_t) + \frac{v_{1t}}{1 - \rho_1 L}$$

where $|\rho_1| < 1$ and $|\rho_2| < 1$. Using (33), we can rewrite this as

$$U_t = U^*(1 - \rho_1)(1 - \rho_2)$$
$$+ (\rho_1 + \rho_2)U_{t-1} - \rho_1\rho_2 U_{t-2} + (1 - \rho_2 L)v_{1t} - \theta(1 - \rho_1 L)\, v_{2t}$$
$$(48)$$

where $v_t$ is a $2 \times 1$ vector white noise with covariance matrix $Ev_t v_t' = V_v$ with diagonal components $\sigma_i$; $L$ is the lag operator.[5] This specification allows separate dynamic responses to $v_{1t}$, the disturbance to the Phillips curve, and to $v_{2t} \equiv y_t - x_t$, the surprise in inflation. For much of this chapter and the next, we shall set $\rho_1 = \rho_2 = 0$ to make some theoretical points. In our empirical work in Chapter 9, we shall permit nonzero $\rho_j$'s.

## Self-confirmation

Self-confirmation reconciles beliefs with the environment. Recall how the Phelps problem is defined in terms of the government's perceived Phillips curve (32) with its arbitrary parameter vector $\gamma$. The following definition makes $\gamma$ an outcome.

DEFINITION: A *self-confirming* equilibrium is a fixed vector $\gamma$ describing government beliefs, a fixed government decision rule $h$ for setting inflation, and an associated stationary stochastic process for $(y_t, U_t, x_t)$ such that

(a) Inflation obeys $y_t = hX_{t-1} + v_{2t}$, where $h = h(\gamma)$. This means that up to the random disturbance $v_{2t}$, inflation solves the Phelps problem.

---

[4] Our specification of the Phillips curve is an adaptation of Chung's (1990).
[5] In this chapter, I assume that $V_v$ is a diagonal matrix. The estimation work in Chapter 9 allows $V_v$ not to be diagonal.

(b) The public sector optimally forecasts inflation: $x_t = hX_{t-1}$.[6]

(c) Unemployment is generated by the natural-rate hypothesis (48).

(d) Government's beliefs $\gamma$ satisfy the orthogonality conditions

$$E\left[U_t - \gamma'X_{Ct}\right]X'_{Ct} = 0. \tag{50}$$

Here $E$ is the mathematical expectation over the equilibrium probability distribution. Condition (d) makes the government's beliefs $\gamma$ depend on the moment matrices $EU_tX'_{Ct}, EX_{Ct}X'_{Ct}$, as dictated by the least squares normal equations. Conditions (a), (b), (c) make these same moment matrices depend on the government's beliefs $\gamma$. The government's beliefs imply behavior that produces data whose moment matrices confirm the government's beliefs.

*Direction of minimization*

Condition (50) records the vector normal equations for least squares estimates of $\gamma$. These normal equations reconcile the government's beliefs with the environment. In the spirit of Chapter 6, the form of (50) emphasizes how a self-confirming equilibrium depends on the government's statistical model. A distinct self-confirming equilibrium results from replacing item (d) with the following alternative, which differs in the direction of minimization imposed on the government's beliefs:

---

[6] The public forms expectations of inflation by fitting a regression model $y_t = \alpha X_{t-1} + \epsilon_{yt}$, where $\epsilon_{yt}$ is a least squares residual that is orthogonal to $X_{t-1}$. Thus, the public's expectation $x_t$ minimizes $E(y_t - x_t)^2$ by choice of the vector $\alpha$ in

$$x_t = \alpha X_{t-1}. \tag{49}$$

Notice that the form of the public's sector's rule coincides with the form of the government's decision rule for setting the predictable part of inflation. In a self-confirming equilibrium, $\alpha = h$.

(d′) Government's beliefs $\gamma$ are obtained by first fitting the Keynesian Phillips curve (35), parameterized by $\beta$, then using the inversion formulas given in (36). The government's estimate of $\beta$ satisfies the orthogonality conditions

$$E\left[y_t - \beta' X_{Kt}\right] X'_{Kt} = 0, \tag{51}$$

and $X_{Kt}$ is defined beneath (35).

Because the government's beliefs affect its behavior and therefore the probability distribution for all observables, the direction of minimization affects outcomes.

Equilibria incorporating either (d) or (d′) close a self-referential loop. The government's beliefs – $\gamma$ or $\beta$ – determine its behavior rule $h(\gamma)$ and the public's forecasting rule. These outcomes determine the stochastic process with respect to which the expectation in (50) or (51) is evaluated.

*Vanishing parameters*

Equilibrium concepts differ in how they make parameters describing expectations appear or disappear. In the original version of the Phelps problem with adaptive expectations, a parameter $\lambda$ describes the public's beliefs. Imposing rational expectations makes this parameter disappear. In the more general Phelps problem, parameters for the public's beliefs are absorbed into the reduced form Phillips curve, whose parameters now summarize the government's model. A self-confirming equilibrium makes parameters describing both the government's and the public's expectations disappear.[7]

The remainder of this chapter describes two types of self-confirming equilibria, links them to the econometric issues raised by King and Watson, and shows their outcomes.

---

[7] Remember Lucas's warning to 'beware of theorists bearing free parameters.'

## *Self-confirmation under classical direction*

A self-confirming equilibrium closes the following circle. The $\gamma$ from the perceived Phillips curve $U_t = \gamma' X_{Ct} + \epsilon_{Ct}$ induces, via the Phelps problem, the decision rule for inflation

$$y_t = h(\gamma)X_{t-1} + v_{2t}.$$

This, in conjunction with formulas for the moments and the normal equations (50), implies that the actual projection of $U_t$ on $X_{Ct}$ is

$$\hat{E}\, U_t|X_{Ct} = T(h)'X_{Ct},$$

where $\hat{E}(\cdot)$ is the linear least squares projection operator, and where $T(h)$ is induced by the normal equations and some moment formulas. A self-confirming equilibrium satisfies:

$$T(h(\gamma)) = \gamma. \tag{52}$$

### *Moment formulas*

By way of characterizing $T(\cdot)$, I describe how to compute a self-confirming equilibrium. To calculate the second moments that appear in (50) under the system as it responds to the government's behavior, I apply elementary formulas for linear stochastic processes (e.g., see Anderson, Hansen, McGrattan, and Sargent (1996)). To describe the motion of the system, add $v_t$ to the state vector. The state for the system is then

$$\bar{X}_t = \begin{bmatrix} v_t \\ X_t \end{bmatrix} = \begin{bmatrix} v_t \\ X_{Ut} \\ X_{yt} \\ 1 \end{bmatrix}.$$

Let $\bar{X}_t$ be the state excluding the constant component 1. Then the motion of the system is

$$\bar{X}_{t+1} = c + \bar{A}\, \bar{X}_t + C v_{t+1}. \tag{53}$$

Let

$$\mu = E\bar{X}_t$$
$$V_{\bar{X}}(0) = E(\bar{X}_t - \mu)(\bar{X}_t - \mu)'$$
$$V_{\bar{X}}(1) = E(\bar{X}_t - \mu)(\bar{X}_{t-1} - \mu)'.$$

Then

$$\mu = (I - \bar{A})^{-1}c \qquad (54a)$$
$$V_{\bar{X}}(0) = \bar{A}V_{\bar{X}}(0)\bar{A}' + CV_v C' \qquad (54b)$$
$$V_{\bar{X}}(1) = \bar{A}V_{\bar{X}}(0), \qquad (54c)$$

where recall that $V_v = E v_t v_t'$.[8] These formulas give all the moments in the normal equations (50) that define the actual regressions used to form the perceived Phillips curve.

## *Keynesian direction of fit*

What the government observes depends partly on what it believes. Studying how the idea of a self-confirming equilibrium interacts with the issues studied by King and Watson provides a practical illustration. This is relevant, because the renaissance of the U.S. Phillips curve stems from an econometric relation with $y_t$ as the left side variable.[9] King and Watson (1994) call this a Keynesian identification scheme for the contemporaneous innovations in a vector autoregression for $y_t, U_t$ because Robert Gordon and Robert Solow used it in widely cited studies.

I assume that the government overlooks the econometric details, sees the Phillips curve handed to it as an exploitable relationship, and solves the Phelps problem. Except for the direction of fit, all other aspects of the model agree with the previous version.

---

[8] Equation (54b) is a discrete Lyapunov or Sylvester equation and can be solved by algorithms described in Anderson, Hansen, McGrattan, and Sargent (1996).

[9] For example, see Jeffrey Fuhrer (1995). When I delivered a talk about this essay at Northwestern University and had finished describing self-confirmation with the classical direction of fit but had not yet presented the setup with the Keynesian direction of fit, Professor Robert Eisner helpfully remarked that the Phillips curve should be run with $y_t$ on the left.

*Government beliefs and behavior*

The econometric department of the government continues to believe in an exploitable Phillips curve of the form (32), but now estimates it by applying least squares to the reverse relationship (35), namely, $y_t = \beta' X_{Kt} + \epsilon_{Kt}$. The normal equations are (51) or $\beta = E(X_{Kt} X'_{Kt})^{-1} E(X_{Kt} y_t)$.

For the Keynesian direction of minimization, a self-confirming equilibrium is defined like the classical one. The estimated Phillips curve (35) implies an inverted Phillips curve

$$U_t = \gamma' X_{Ct} + \tilde{\epsilon}_{2t}, \tag{55}$$

with associated $\gamma(\beta) = [\gamma_1 \ \gamma'_{-1}] = [\beta_1^{-1} \quad - \beta'_{-1}/\beta_1]$; this is used in the Phelps problem to set the actual rate of inflation

$$y_t = h X_{t-1} + v_{2t}, \tag{56}$$

where $h = h(\gamma)$ solves the Phelps problem. Via formulas (54), this makes the actual projection of $y_t$ on $X_{Kt}$, i.e., the actual Keynesian Phillips curve, become

$$\hat{E} y_t \mid X_{Kt} = S(h)' X_{Kt}.$$

A self-confirming equilibrium satisfies $S(h(\gamma(\beta))) = \beta$.

*Calculation of S*

Under the Keynesian identification scheme, it is easy to compute the operator $S(\beta)$ mapping the government's believed Phillips curve into the one that would be recovered by least squares in a large sample. Let $\hat{\beta} \equiv S(\beta)$. Express (56) as

$$y_t = \begin{bmatrix} 0 \\ h \end{bmatrix}' X_{Kt} + v_{2t},$$

substitute into the normal equation (51) and rearrange to get

$$E X_{Kt} \left( \begin{bmatrix} 0 \\ h \end{bmatrix}' X_{Kt} - \hat{\beta}' X_{Kt} + v_{2t} \right) = 0;$$

$v_{2t}$ is orthogonal to all components of $X_{kt}$ except for $U_t$, with which its covariance is from (48) equal to $-\theta\sigma_2^2$. Here $h$ is implicitly a function of $\beta$, via the Phelps problem. Then the normal equations imply

$$S(\beta) = \hat{\beta} = \begin{bmatrix} 0 \\ h \end{bmatrix} + \phi \qquad (57a)$$

where

$$\phi = \left( E X_{Kt} X'_{Kt} \right)^{-1} \begin{bmatrix} -\theta\sigma_2^2 \\ 0 \end{bmatrix}. \qquad (57b)$$

*Special case by hand*

It is instructive to consider the special case where $\rho_1 = \rho_2 = 0$, which lets each of the self-confirming equilibria be computed by hand. The government's problem collapses to a sequence of static problems, independently of $\delta$.[10] Accordingly, we take $X_{t-1} = 1$. The Phillips curve (48), the condition that $v_{1t}$ is orthogonal to the right side variables, and the rest of the specification imply

$$\text{var}(U_t) = \theta^2\sigma_2^2 + \sigma_1^2$$
$$\text{var}(y_t) = \sigma_2^2 \qquad (58)$$
$$\text{cov}(U_t, y_t) = -\theta\sigma_2^2.$$

For the classical direction of fit ($U_t$ on $y_t$),

$$\gamma_1 = \frac{\text{cov}(U_t, y_t)}{\text{var}(y_t)} = -\theta.$$

To determine the constant $\gamma_{-1}$, I use information about the government's decision rule. By solving the first-order conditions for the government's problem, we find

$$\hat{y}_t = x_t = \frac{-\gamma_{-1}\gamma_1}{\gamma_1^2 + 1},$$

---

[10] This observation rationalizes the control problem studied by Sims (1988).

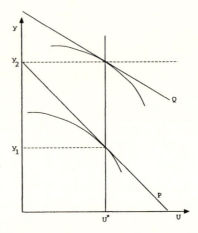

**Figure 7.1.** Two self-confirming
equilibria.

which is a constant, call it $\bar{x}$. Because the means lie on the
regression line, use the formula for $\bar{x}$ to compute $\gamma_{-1} = (\gamma_1^2 +$
$1)U^*$. For the Keynesian direction of fit ($y_t$ on $U_t$), we have
$\beta_1 = \frac{-\theta\sigma_2^2}{\sigma_1^2 + \theta^2\sigma_2^2}$. The government now computes its rule using the
Phillips curve $U_t = \frac{-\beta_{-1}}{\beta_1} + \beta_1^{-1}y_t$, which implies that $\hat{y}_t = \frac{\beta_{-1}}{\beta_1^2 + 1} =$
$\bar{x}$, a constant. Imposing $\bar{x} = \beta_{-1} + \beta_1 U^*$ implies that $\beta_{-1} =$
$\frac{-\beta_1^2 + 1}{\beta_1} U^*$. This then implies that in the perceived Phillips curve,
$\gamma_{-1} = \frac{\beta_1^2 + 1}{\beta_1^2} U^*$.

I compute a numerical example depicted in Figure 7.1. I take
an economy with $\theta = 1, U^* = 5, \sigma_1 = .3, \sigma_2 = .3$. The classical form of self-confirming equilibrium has $\gamma_{-1} = U^*(1 + \theta^2) =$
$10, \gamma_1 = -\theta = -1$. The mean levels of unemployment and inflation are $(5, 5)$ in this economy. For the Keynesian form, I com-
pute $\beta_{-1} = 12.5, \beta_1 = -.5$, and $\gamma_{-1} = 25, \gamma_1 = -2$. The mean
levels of unemployment and inflation in the self-confirming
equilibrium are now $(5, 10)$. The government's decision rule

for inflation is simply $\hat{y}_t = 10$. In Figure 7.1, curve P is the self-confirming Phillips curve estimated with the classical direction of fit. Curve Q is the self-confirming Phillips curve estimated with the Keynesian direction of fit. Under the classical direction of fit, the inflation and unemployment on average are the Nash equilibrium pair $(y_1, U^*)$. Under the Keynesian direction, the Phillips curve is estimated to be flatter, and the inflation rate is on average higher, at $y_2$.

The example shows how the direction of minimization affects the outcome. With the Keynesian direction, the government believes a larger constant and a larger effect of inflation on unemployment in the $U_t$-on-$y_t$ relationship. Because this makes the government believe that the Phillips curve trade-off is more favorable than it is, it sets inflation twice as high. See Figure 7.1.

### Why not Ramsey?

Each of these two computed self-confirming equilibria gives a mean outcome worse than the Ramsey outcome. This signifies a breakdown in one of the hypotheses of the Chapter 5 Proposition that the solution of the Phelps problem eventually sustains nearly a Ramsey outcome. What fails is the induction hypothesis restricting the sum of the weights on lagged inflation (either zero on current and lagged inflation in the classical version or one on lagged inflation in the Keynesian version).[11] In the examples, because $\rho_1 = \rho_2 = 0$, the self-confirming equilibria are serially uncorrelated processes for $U_t, y_t$, making lagged $(U_t, y_t)$'s disappear from empirical Phillips curves. Deactivating the induction hypothesis makes the government in effect solve a one-period problem, and shuts down the intertemporal avenue that promotes better outcomes in the Proposition. This is relevant for the simulations in the following chapter.

---

[11] These two example self-confirming equilibria exhibit the assertion of Lucas (1972) and Sargent (1971) that rational expectations and the natural-rate hypothesis do not imply the induction hypothesis.

*Direction of minimization: caution*

The outcomes of our two self-confirming equilibria depend on details of the stochastic specifications, and in particular, the orthogonality of the disturbance $v_t$ to the other right side variables in the true expectational Phillips curve (48), and the orthogonality of $v_{2t}$ to $\hat{y}_t$ in the inflation generator (33). These orthogonality conditions make our first self-confirming equilibrium on average recover the Nash outcome. The classical identifying conditions are more consistent with the environment, and this helps account for the better average outcome under the classical identification.

Evidently, it would be possible to affect the quality of outcomes in the two self-confirming equilibria by appropriately altering the assumed orthogonality conditions in (48). My purpose at this point is not to recommend one set of orthogonality conditions over another in (48), but to point out their influence on outcomes. In this way, though our behavioral model of the government differs from theirs, we are joining King and Watson's (1994) inquiry.

*Equilibrium computation*

Depending on the direction of fit, a self-confirming equilibrium is either the fixed point $\gamma = T(h(\gamma))$ for the classical direction or $\beta = S(h(\gamma(\beta)))$ for the Keynesian direction. To conserve notation at a cost of an inconsistency, I shall occasionally denote these two mappings as $T(\gamma)$ and $S(\beta)$, respectively. In practice, an equilibrium can be calculated by employing the relaxation algorithm

$$\beta_{j+1} = \kappa\beta_j + (1-\kappa)S(\beta_j), \tag{59}$$

where $\kappa \in [0,1)$ is the relaxation parameter. It is useful sometimes to represent (59) as the adaptive scheme

$$\beta_{j+1} = \beta_j + (1-\kappa)[S(\beta_j) - \beta_j]. \tag{60}$$

When $\kappa = 0$, (59) is equivalent to iterating on $S$. Setting $\kappa > 0$ can assist convergence. Notice the resemblance of (60) to the recursive representation of the least squares algorithm (8). In the next chapter, I transform the equilibrium computation algorithm (60) into real time dynamics for the government's beliefs by making the government estimate the Phillips curve recursively using the most recent data.

## Messages

Self-confirming equilibria impose rational expectations by requiring the public to use an unimprovable forecasting scheme. [12] Different self-confirming equilibria attribute separate quantitative theories – really identification schemes – to the government. Those lead to different policies. The next chapter shows how least squares learning impels the system toward some self-confirming equilibrium but how it need not dispel an erroneous identification scheme nor lead to a Nash equilibrium outcome.

## Equilibrium with misspecified beliefs

Readers of Kalai and Lehrer (1993) might have foreseen that the self-confirming equilibrium under classical identification puts the mean inflation rate at the Nash outcome. The result reflects convergence to the truth when decision makers' probability models encompass the Nash equilibrium. The classical identification scheme satisfies the required encompassing condition. But the Keynesian identification scheme gives the government a mistaken interpretation of the contemporaneous covariance between innovations to inflation and unemployment, and that worsens outcomes relative to the Nash outcome.

To explore how imputing a different wrong model might improve upon the Nash outcome, I now propose a model in which the public, not the government, makes a subtle specification error. This model links adaptive expectations, the induction hypothesis, and the Phelps problem. It will be useful in identifying

[12] The public forecasts with a conditional expectations over the equilibrium distribution.

features that will help interpret some simulations and empirical estimates.

The model has a misspecification like the one we put into Bray's model. Within the class of exponential smoothing forecasting rules, the public's beliefs must be optimal, just as in our modification of Bray's model.

### An erroneous forecasting function

The government knows the correct model, but not the public. The government's model is

$$U_t = U^* - \theta(y_t - x_t) + v_{1t}$$
$$x_t = Cy_{t-1} + (1 - C)x_{t-1}, \quad C \in (0, 1). \tag{61}$$

We continue to assume that $v_t$ is a $2 \times 1$ vector white noise. The public has adaptive expectations but tunes the free parameter to fit the data. Thus, $C$ will be determined as a fixed point of an operator mapping beliefs into optimal beliefs. By choice of a linear decision rule for $y_t$, the government solves the Phelps problem: maximize the criterion function

$$-E_0 \sum_{t=0}^{\infty} \delta^t [(U^* - \theta(y_t - x_t))^2 + y_t^2]$$

subject to the second equation of (61), with $x_t$ being taken as a state variable, and $y_t$ as the control. The optimum is a feedback rule

$$y_t = f_1 + f_2 x_t + v_{2t},$$

which has noise because the government cannot perfectly control inflation.

The government's behavior makes the actual rate of inflation

$$y_t = \frac{f_1}{1 - f_2} + \frac{1 - (1 - C)L}{1 - (1 - C(1 - f_2))L} v_{2t}. \tag{62}$$

This can be written

$$y_t = \nu + h(L)v_{2t}, \tag{63}$$

so that the true process has mean $\nu$ and spectrum

$$F(\omega; C) = h(\exp(i\omega))h(\exp(-i\omega))\sigma_2^2. \tag{64}$$

This reasoning induces a mapping from $C$ to $F(\omega; C)$, via the Phelps problem.

Given $C$ and a process of the form (62), we seek the best fitting model of the form

$$y_t = \frac{1 - (1 - c)L}{1 - L}\epsilon_t \tag{65}$$

or

$$y_t = g(L)\epsilon_t. \tag{66}$$

The free parameters in (65) are $c, \sigma_\epsilon^2$. The process has mean 0 and spectrum

$$G(\omega) = g(\exp(i\omega))g(\exp(-i\omega))\sigma_\epsilon^2.$$

Notice that $G(\omega)$ depends on $c$, through $g(\exp(i\omega))$. As in our analysis of Bray's model, given $C$ and therefore (62), we can find the least squares value of $c$ for the model (65).[13] The Phelps problem and the approximation problem thereby induce a best estimate mapping, $c = B(C)$. We define an equilibrium under forecast misspecification as a fixed point of $B$. This definition makes both the true and the approximating models equilibrium outcomes.

---

[13] Again, the best approximating $c, \sigma_\epsilon^2$ can be computed by minimizing with respect to $c, \sigma_\epsilon^2$ the expression (47) given above.

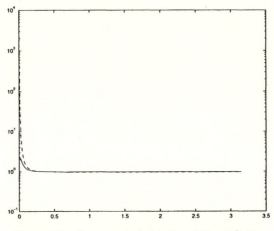

**Figure 7.2.** Log spectral density of the inflation for the true (solid) and misspecified (dotted line) models, $\delta = .97$.

Figure 7.2 shows the log spectra for inflation for the equilibrium true and approximating models, for the parameter values $U^* = 5, \theta = 1, \sigma_1 = \sigma_2 = .3, \delta = .97$. Associated equilibrium values are $C = .0673, \sigma_\epsilon = 1.0155, f_1 = 1.0243, f_2 = .3495$. The one-step ahead standard error of prediction for the true model is 1, compared with 1.0134 for the approximating model.

### *Approaching Ramsey*

The most important outcome is that the implied mean inflation rate is 1.57, substantially down from the Nash value of 5. Calculations confirm that as $\delta$ approaches 1 from below, the mean inflation rate approaches the Ramsey value 0.[14] The true and approximating spectral densities match well at all but low frequencies. The true inflation rate is only moderately serially

---

[14] For values of $\delta = (.95, .96, .98, .99)$ equilibrium values are, respectively, $C = (.079, .074, .059, .019)$, $\sigma_\epsilon = (1.0182, 1.017, 1.0135, 1.0032)$, and mean inflation equal $(2.00, 1.80, 1.29, .25)$.

correlated, as indicated by the modest departure from the perfectly flat spectral density that characterizes a serially uncorrelated process. As in the Bray model, by simulating a mean with a unit root, the approximating model is using second moment properties to capture first moments.

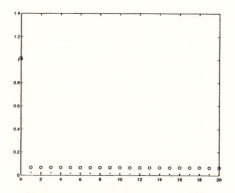

**Figure 7.3.** Impulse response functions for true (dots) and approximating (circles) models, $\delta = .97$. The circle at zero lag is just above a dot at zero lag at value 1.

Figure 7.3 reports impulse response functions for the true and approximating models. A unit root manifests itself in a nonzero asymptote in the impulse response for the approximating model.

This example separates the equilibrium true and approximating models only at very low frequencies. Figure 1 suggests that it would take many observations for the people living inside this model to detect that their model is wrong. Nevertheless, the average inflation outcome coming from this model is very different from the Nash outcome (i.e., 1.6 versus 5). The induction hypothesis incorporated in the adaptive expectations scheme and the high discount factor of $\delta = .97$ deliver the improved outcome. Because $C$ is an outcome, the present model sharpens our earlier account of the workings of the induction hypothesis in the Phelps problem by removing $C$ as a parameter that can be manipulated independently of $\delta$.

*Grounds for optimism*

After disappointments from our self confirming equilibria, the equilibrium with forecast misspecification is heartening in supporting better than Nash outcomes. The equilibrium concept is not self-confirming, but has that spirit. It embodies a type of self-confirmation with a wrong model. That the approximation error in our example is small shows that there is a nearly self-confirming model with much better than Nash outcomes.

We take this optimism and the mechanism that generates it into the next chapter, where we construct adaptive versions of our self-confirming models.

# 8
## *Adaptive Expectations (1990's)*

### *Least squares adaptation*

This chapter modifies self-confirming equilibria to attain adaptive models in the style of Sims (1988) and Chung (1990) and studies whether they converge to self-confirming equilibria. I withhold knowledge of population regressions from agents, and require them to learn by updating least squares regressions as time passes. The government sets the inflation rate at the first-period recommendation of the Phelps problem for its current estimate of the Phillips curve.[1]

Starting from the self-confirming equilibrium models of Chapter 7, we in effect alter a free parameter that determines a gain sequence governing the rate at which past observations are discounted. If the gain is set to implement least squares learning, we eventually get nothing new from these models because under suitable assumptions on parameter values, they converge to self-confirming equilibria and leave us stuck at the Nash equilibrium outcome. However, if we set a constant gain, making agents discount past observations, new outcomes can emerge. Agents' discounting of past observations arrests convergence to a self-confirming equilibrium and can sustain paths that look like Volcker terminating inflation.

A purpose of this chapter is to replicate, analyze, and reinterpret simulations like those of Chung (1990) and Sims (1988). I add two things to their work. First, I relate their systems to the self-confirming equilibria of Chapter 7, and apply theorems

---

[1] Appendix B relates this type of adaptive model to Kreps's idea of anticipated utility.

from the literature on least squares learning to determine the limiting behavior of the models under alternative specifications of the government's adaptation algorithm.[2] Second, I interpret the behavior of the simulations in terms of recurrent dynamics that escape a self-confirming equilibrium and sustain close to Ramsey outcomes during long episodes. These escapes reflect how the approximating models use a unit root to approximate a constant and are reminiscent of Chapter 7's equilibrium with misspecified forecasting.

Before presenting the details of our adaptive models, the next section provides an overview of the issues and the analytical methods.

## *Primer on recursive algorithms*

Within a compact notation, this section introduces the main concepts of this chapter and describes how our adaptive models connect to self-confirming equilibria.

A self-confirming equilibrium is determined by a government's beliefs about some population moments and associated regression coefficients. For the classical identification scheme, these beliefs are measured by $(\gamma, EX_C X'_C, EUX_C)$. Time $t$ values of these are among the economy's state variables in the adaptive models of this chapter. They disappear as state variables in a self-confirming equilibrium because they are constants.

A self-confirming equilibrium under the classical identification satisfies a set of moment conditions

$$ER_{XC}^{-1}(\gamma) \left[ U_t X'_{Ct} - (X_{Ct} X_{Ct})' \gamma \right] = 0 \qquad (67a)$$

$$EX_{Ct} X'_{Ct} - R_{XC}(\gamma) = 0, \qquad (67b)$$

where the mathematical expectation is taken with respect to a distribution of $(U_t, X_{Ct})$ that depends on $\gamma$ through the solution

---

[2] See Evans and Honkapohja's (1998b) handbook chapter and their forthcoming monograph (1998c) for comprehensive treatments of learning in macroeconomics.

$h(\gamma)$ of the Phelps problem. Self-reference surfaces in the dependence of this distribution on $\gamma$. For convenience, assemble the unknowns into the vector

$$\phi = \begin{bmatrix} \gamma \\ \mathrm{col}(R_{XC}) \end{bmatrix},$$

where $\mathrm{col}(R_{XC})$ is a vector formed by stacking the columns of $R_{XC}$. The moment equations can be written as

$$E\left[F(\phi, \zeta)\right] = 0, \tag{68}$$

where $\zeta$ is a random vector. For arbitrary $\phi$, define

$$b(\phi) = E\left[F(\phi, \zeta)\right]. \tag{69}$$

A self-confirming equilibrium has a set of beliefs $\phi_f$ satisfying

$$b(\phi_f) = 0. \tag{70}$$

The next subsections describe alternative recursive algorithms for solving (70). A change of perspective converts these computational algorithms into models of real-time adaptation.

*Iteration*

Compute a sequence $\{\phi_k\}$ of estimates of $\phi$ from

$$\phi_{k+1} = \phi_k + ab(\phi_k), \tag{71}$$

where the distribution used for evaluating the expectation defining $b(\phi_k)$ in (68) is evaluated at the estimate $\phi_k$, and $a > 0$ is a step size. This represents the iterative algorithm described in chapter 7. Each step requires evaluating the mathematical expectation $b(\phi) = E\left[F(\phi, \zeta)\right]$, the reason we reported the moment formulas in chapter 7.

*Stochastic approximations*

A random version of (71) can be obtained by substituting $F(\phi_n, \zeta_n)$ for its mean $b(\phi_n)$ and manipulating the step size to perform the averaging. In particular, compute the stochastic process

$$\phi_{n+1} = \phi_n + a_n F(\phi_n, \zeta), \qquad (72)$$

where $\{a_n\}$ is a positive sequence of scalars satisfying

$$a_n > 0, \quad \sum_{n=0}^{\infty} a_n = +\infty. \qquad (73)$$

Define artificial time

$$t_n = \sum_{k=0}^{n} a_k \qquad (74)$$

and form the sampled processes $\phi(t_n) = \phi_n$. Interpolate $\phi(t_n)$ to get a continuous time process $\phi^o(t)$ (typically a piecewise linear interpolation). Then obtain a continuous time process that approximates $\phi^o(t)$ as $n \to +\infty$ and use it to study the limiting behavior of the original $\phi_n$ process (72).

We get different approximating processes by adjusting the rate of decrease of the gain sequence $\{a_n\}$ in (73). Different gain sequences affect details of the approximation through the mapping (74) from real discrete time $n$ to artificial time $t_n$.

*Mean dynamics*

Classic stochastic approximation algorithms (Kushner and Clark (1978) and Ljung (1977)) set $a_n \sim \frac{1}{n}$ (at least $\forall\, t \geq N$ for some $N > 0$). That permits strong statements about the almost sure convergence of (72) to a zero of $b(\phi)$. For $a_n \sim \frac{1}{n}$, as $n \to \infty$, the stochastic process $\phi^o(t)$ approaches the solution of an ordinary differential equation

$$\frac{d\phi^o(t)}{dt} = b(\phi^o). \qquad (75)$$

Equation (75) generates the mean dynamics. Using an argument sketched in the appendix to Chapter 3, when $a_n \sim \frac{1}{n}$, a law of large numbers makes the random term in the continuous time approximation converge to zero fast enough that the mean dynamics (75) describe the tail behavior of the stochastic process $\phi_n$ in (72). If the algorithm (almost surely) converges, it is to a zero of the mean dynamics, $0 = b(\phi)$, a self-confirming equilibrium. The ODE contains information about the local and global stability of the algorithm (72). We present and analyze this ODE for some examples later in this chapter.[3]

*Constant gain*

We are also interested in versions of the algorithm (72) with $a_n = \epsilon > 0 \; \forall n$. Limit theorems about such constant gain algorithms use a weaker notion of convergence (convergence in distribution) than those for the classic stochastic approximation, where $a_n \sim \frac{1}{n}$ facilitates almost sure convergence. With a constant gain $a_n = \epsilon$, limit theorems are about small noise limits as $\epsilon \to 0$ and as $n\epsilon \to +\infty$.

Again define artificial time using (74) and form a family of processes

$$\phi_{n+1}^\epsilon = \phi_n^\epsilon + \epsilon F(\phi_n^\epsilon, \zeta_n). \qquad (76)$$

Form $\phi^\epsilon(t)$ by interpolating $\phi^\epsilon(t_n)$, and study small $\epsilon$ limits of the family. Kushner and Dupuis (1987), Kushner and Yin (1997), and Gulinsky and Veretennikov (1993) verified conditions under which as $\epsilon \to 0$ and $\epsilon n \to \infty$, the $\phi_n^\epsilon$ process converges in distribution to the zeros of the mean dynamics (75). The restrictions on the mean dynamics (75) needed for convergence match those from the classic stochastic approximation ($a_n \sim \frac{1}{n}$) theory.

---

[3] See Brock and LeBaron (1996) Brock and Hommes (1997) for models driven by stable mean dynamics far from rational expectations equilibria and by locally unstable adaptation near them.

*Escape routes*

Another use of the constant gain apparatus is more pertinent for this chapter, namely, the application of the theory of large deviations to characterize excursions of (76) away from $\phi_f$. The main purpose of this chapter is to study outcomes that emerge when the government is endowed with a constant-gain learning algorithm that impedes convergence to a self-confirming equilibrium. We are as interested in movements away from a self-confirming equilibrium as in those toward one.

The theory of large deviations characterizes excursions away from $\phi_f$ by using the following objects: a log moment generating function of an averaged version of the innovation process $F(\phi_n, \zeta_n)$; the Legendre transform of that log moment generating function; and an action functional defined in terms of the Legendre transformation. Where $\theta$ is a vector conformable to $F$, the log moment generating function $H(\theta, \phi)$ is designed to approximate[4]

$$H(\theta, \phi) = \log E \exp \left( \theta' F(\phi, \zeta) \right). \tag{77}$$

Here the mathematical expectation $E$ is taken over the distribution of $\zeta$. The Legendre transform of $H$ is

$$L(\beta, \phi) = \sup_{\theta}[\theta' \beta - H(\theta, \phi)]. \tag{78}$$

---

[4] See Dupuis and Kushner (1987, p. 225) and Kushner and Yin (1997, p. 275) for the technical details. They assume that for each $\delta > 0$, the following limit exists uniformly in $\phi_i, \alpha_i$ in any compact set:

$$\sum_{i=0}^{T/\delta-1} \delta H(\alpha_i, \phi_i) = \lim_{N} \frac{\delta}{N} \log E \exp \sum_{i=0}^{T/\delta-1} \alpha_i' \sum_{j=iN}^{iN+N-1} F(\phi_i, \zeta_j).$$

The action functional $S(T, \phi)$ is

$$S(T,\phi) = \begin{cases} \int_0^T L\left(\frac{d}{ds}\phi(s), \phi(s)\right) ds & \text{if } \phi(s) \text{ is abs. cts. and } \phi(0) = \phi_f; \\ \infty & \text{otherwise.} \end{cases} \quad (79)$$

Dupuis and Kushner describe a deterministic programming problem for finding the escape route along which paths of the algorithm move away from a self-confirming equilibrium $\phi_f$. Let $D$ be a compact set containing $\phi_f$. Let $\partial D$ be the boundary of this set. Let $C[0, T]$ be the space of continuous functions $\phi(t)$ on the interval $[0, T]$. The escape route $\phi(t)$ solves:

$$\inf_{T>0} \inf_{\phi \in A} S(T, \phi) \qquad (80)$$

where

$$A = \{\phi(\cdot) \in C[0, T], \phi(T) \in \partial D\}.$$

Assume that the minimizer $\tilde{\phi}(\cdot)$ is unique, and let $t_D^\epsilon$ be the time that $\phi^\epsilon(t)$ first leaves $D$. Dupuis and Kushner (1987, p. 242) show that for all $\delta > 0$,

$$\lim_{\epsilon \to 0} \text{Prob}\left(|\phi^\epsilon(t_D^\epsilon) - \tilde{\phi}(T)| > \delta\right) = 0. \qquad (81)$$

While the mean dynamics don't depend on the noise around the mean dynamics, the escape routes do. Not only do the noises add random fluctuations around (75); they contribute another set of paths, the escape routes.[5] The most interesting features of the simulations below come from movements along escape routes.

*Simplification of action functional*

While the escape route calculations promise cheap information about central tendencies of our stochastic algorithms, it can be difficult to calculate the action functional (79). There

[5] See Freidlin and Wentzell (1984), especially chapter 4, and Dupuis and Kushner (1985, 1989).

are specializations and modifications of the algorithm (72) that simplify the action functional. A most important one makes $F(\phi, \zeta) = b(\phi) + \sigma(\phi)\zeta$, where $\zeta_n$ is stationary and Gaussian, but not necessarily serially uncorrelated. Define $R = \sum_j E\zeta_t\zeta_{t-j}$ Then Dupuis and Kushner[6] report the following formula for the action functional:

$$S(T, \phi) = .5 \int_0^T \left(\frac{d}{ds}\phi - b(\phi)\right)' \left[\sigma(\phi)R\sigma(\phi)'\right]^+ \left(\frac{d}{ds}\phi - b(\phi)\right) h(s)ds \quad (82)$$

where $(\cdot)^+$ is the generalized inverse (used to get around possible stochastic singularity).[7]

### From computation to adaptation

While the preceding description treats the recursive formulas for $\phi$ as algorithms to approximate a self-confirming equilibrium, the same mathematics tell what we can get from modifying our models of self-confirming equilibrium to incorporate adaptation. Key facts for us are: (1) gain sequences that implement versions of least squares make the mean dynamics pull the economy toward self-confirming equilibria; (2) gain sequences that fall off more slowly than least squares, and thereby discount the past faster, increase the frequency with which escape dynamics influence outcomes.[8]

---

[6] See Dupuis and Kushner, 1985, especially the remark on the top of page 678. See also Kushner and Clark (1978) and Kushner and Yin (1992) for descriptions of K-W algorithms.

[7] The function $h(s)$ depends on the form of the gain function; for example, $h(s) = \exp s$ if $\gamma = 1$ in $a_n = a_0/(n^\gamma)$, and $h(s) = 1$ if $\gamma < 1$. See Dupuis and Kushner (1989, p. 1113.) Also see Kushner and Yin (1997, chapter 10).

[8] Here is a brief history of the ideas in this section. Lucas and Prescott (1971) dismissed iterating on (70) as a computational strategy, but Townsend (1983) used it. Woodford (1990) and Marcet and Sargent (1989a, 1989b) used the mean dynamics (75) associated with a stochastic approximation algorithm to establish conditions for the convergence of least squares learning to rational expectations in models with self-reference. Both Woodford and Marcet and Sargent required continuity of $b(\phi)$. In-Koo Cho (1997a, 1997b) studied problems with discontinuous $b(\phi)$ inherited from discontinuous decision rules (e.g., trigger strategies in

## Adaptation with the classical identification

In a self-confirming equilibrium, the government solves the Phelps problem only at the equilibrium values of its perceived Phillips curve and implements the recommendations of a unique Phelps rule as time passes. In contrast, I now assume that the government solves a new Phelps problem and uses a different decision rule each period as it adapts to new information about the Phillips curve.[9]

### *The government's beliefs and behavior*

The government arrives at time $t$ with a model (32) and an estimate $\gamma_{t-1}$ of the coefficients $\gamma$. It sets the systematic part of inflation $\hat{y}_t$ by solving the Phelps problem with $\gamma = \gamma_{t-1}$. This produces the outcome [10]

$$y_t = h(\gamma_{t-1})X_{t-1} + v_{2t}. \tag{83}$$

In forming $\hat{y}_t = h(\gamma_{t-1})X_{t-1}$, the government acts at $t$ as if its model for the Phillips curve for all $j \geq 0$ is

$$U_{t+j} = \gamma_{t-1}X_{C,t+j} + \varepsilon_{C,t+j}. \tag{84}$$

models of credibility and search problems). To make least squares learning approach rational expectations, he used algorithms with $\frac{1}{\log n} < a_n < \frac{1}{\sqrt{n}}$. This led to a diffusion approximation to (72). For Cho's settings, the assumptions about gains that lead to the diffusion approximation are important in promoting sufficient experimentation to discover a rational expectations equilibrium. Cho obtained convergence in distribution to rational expectations by driving the weight on the noise term to zero. Kandori, Mailath, and Rob (1993) use related mathematics. Roger Myerson (1998) used an escape route calculation in a voting problem.

[9] The government behaves adaptively in the sense that it updates $\gamma_t$ recursively via least squares, but forms its decisions using the same mapping $h(\cdot)$ of $\gamma_t$ that was appropriate (i.e., optimal given its beliefs) in a self-confirming equilibrium in which $\gamma$ was time invariant. This is what control scientists mean when they speak of (suboptimal) adaptive control, and is an example of Kreps's anticipated utility.

[10] For alternative ways to set up problems like this using active control, where the decision maker balances control and experimentation, see Edward C. Prescott (1967), Volker Wreiland (1995), and Kenneth Kasa (1996).

The content of (84) is that in forecasting the future at $t$, the government pretends that the coefficients $\gamma_{t-1}$ will forever govern the dynamics.

The government's procedure for reestimation falsifies this pretense as it updates $\gamma_t$ via the recursive least squares algorithm (RLS)

$$\gamma_t = \gamma_{t-1} + g_t R_{XC,t}^{-1} X_{Ct} \left( U_t - \gamma_{t-1}' X_{Ct} \right) \qquad (85a)$$

$$R_{XC,t} = R_{XC,t-1} + g_t \left( X_{Ct} X_{Ct}' - R_{XC,t-1} \right). \qquad (85b)$$

In (85), $\{g_t\}$ is a gain sequence of positive scalars. Formula (85) is a stochastic approximation algorithm that is a good method for estimating a $\gamma$ that satisfies the moment conditions $E X_{Ct}(U_t - \gamma' X_{Ct}) = 0$ from (50) if $(X_{Ct}, U_t)$ form a stationary stochastic process. The right side of equation (85a) is a weighting matrix ($R_{XC,t}^{-1}$) times the one-period value of the object $X_{Ct}(U_t - \gamma X_{Ct})$, whose expected value the orthogonality conditions set to zero. Equation (85b) is a recursive algorithm for estimating the second moment matrix of the regressors $X_{Ct}$. We obtain different models of learning with alternative gain sequences. For least squares, $g_t = 1/t$. So-called constant gain algorithms set $g_t = g_o > 0$ and thereby discount past observations. Discounting past observations is a good idea when the government believes that the Phillips curve wanders over time.

### RLS and the Kalman filter

Alternative gain sequences $\{g_t\}$ affect the motion over time of the coefficients $\gamma$ and can be interpreted in terms of connections between RLS and the Kalman filter. These connections are spelled out in an Appendix A. The Kalman filter uses Bayes' law to update beliefs about a hidden Gaussian state variable – in this case $\gamma$ – as observations accrue. Recursive least squares corresponds to a special setting of parameter values when the Kalman filter is applied to the random-walk-in-coefficients model

$$\tilde{\gamma}_t = \tilde{\gamma}_{t-1} + w_t \qquad (86)$$

where $\tilde{\gamma}$ is the value of the parameter in the time varying version of the model

$$U_t = \tilde{\gamma}_t' X_{Ct} + \varepsilon_{Ct} \tag{87}$$

where $E w_t w_t' = R_{1t}, E \varepsilon_{Ct}^2 = R_{2t}; E \epsilon_{Ct} \epsilon_{Cs} = 0$ for $t \neq s$; $E \epsilon_{Ct} v_s = 0$ for all $t$ and $s$; and $E w_t w_s' = 0$ for all $t \neq s$. The Kalman filter assumes that beliefs are summarized by (86), (87); by given sequences of variances $\{R_{1t}, R_{2t}\}_{t \geq 1}$; and by initial conditions for $\gamma_0 = E \tilde{\gamma}_0$, $P_0 = E(\gamma_0 - \tilde{\gamma}_0)(\gamma_0 - \tilde{\gamma}_0)'$. The filter also assumes that $(\{w_t\}, \{\varepsilon_t\}, x_0)$ are jointly Gaussian. The Kalman filter is a recursive formula for $\gamma_t = E \tilde{\gamma}_t | J_t$, where $J_t$ is the sigma algebra generated by observations through date $t$; and a recursive formula for $P_t = E(\gamma_t - \tilde{\gamma}_t)(\gamma_t - \tilde{\gamma}_t)'$. For our application, the information set $J_t$ is the history $[U_s, y_s, s \leq t]$.

The RLS algorithm with a decreasing gain $g_t = \frac{1}{t}$ corresponds to the Kalman filter under the specification $R_{1t} \equiv 0$ and $R_{2t}$ being set to a constant. The RLS with a constant gain $g_t = g_o$ corresponds to a Kalman filter under the specification that $R_{1t} = \left(\frac{g_o}{1-g_o}\right) P_{t-1}$, $R_{2t}$ a constant. These comparisons describe the government's model uncertainty and are useful when we choose initial conditions for some simulations below.

*Private sector beliefs*

There are two convenient ways to model the public's beliefs in an adaptive model under the classical identification scheme for the Phillips curve. One is to follow Sims (1988) and Chung (1990) and let the public know the government's rule $h(\gamma_{t-1})$ at each $t$. Another would be to let the public also use a recursive least squares algorithm to estimate $\alpha_t$ each period in the public's forecasting model $y_t = \alpha_{t-1} X_{t-1} + e_{yt}$. The RLS algorithm would be

$$\alpha_t = \alpha_{t-1} + \ell_t R_{X,t}^{-1} X_t (y_t - \alpha_{t-1}' X_t) \tag{88a}$$

$$R_{X,t} = R_{X,t-1} + \ell_t (X_t X_t' - R_{X,t-1}), \tag{88b}$$

where $\{\ell_t\}$ is another gain sequence.

An advantage of assuming that the public knows $h(\gamma_{t-1})$ is that it eliminates $\alpha_{t-1}$ from the state of the system. We shall work with this reduced system. We can interpret it as the outcome of a system with Fed watchers who give the public an accurate estimate of the government's decision rule at each $t$.

*System evolution*

The dynamic system is completed by the law of motion that determines $(U_t, y_t)$. The adaptive version of the model under the classical identification scheme assumes that unemployment continues to be determined by (48), but now inflation is determined by $y_t = h(\gamma_{t-1}) + v_{2t}$, instead of $y_t = h(\gamma) + v_{2t}$. This means that the entire system can be written in the form (53) with the amendment that $\gamma_{t-1}$ appears on the right side at $t$, replacing $\gamma$. Under the assumption that the public knows the government's rule, the system formed by (85) and this adaptive counterpart to (48) is a stochastic difference equation in the variables $\left[\gamma_{t-1}, R_{XC,t-1}, U_t, y_t\right]$. The components $\left[\gamma_{t-1}, R_{XC,t-1}\right]$ of the system summarize the government's beliefs.

We want to study two aspects of the adaptive system: (1) the potential limit points of these beliefs under a learning rule with a gain that eventually behaves like $\frac{1}{t}$; and (2) how the system behaves under a constant gain learning rule. The mean dynamics determine what we know about $\frac{1}{t}$ gains. If they exist, the limit points are self-confirming equilibria. The escape route dynamics provide the interesting new behavior under constant gain algorithms. We mainly rely on computer simulations to study the constant gain dynamics.

*Mean dynamics*

Stochastic approximation methods deliver an ordinary differential equation (ODE) whose behavior about a fixed point contains much information about the limiting behavior of the stochastic difference equations governing our adaptive system. The ODE can be derived mechanically by imitating the steps we used in applying Margaret Bray's idea to our model in Chapter 3.[11]

Application of those steps to the system formed by (85) and the adaptive version of (48) leads to the ordinary differential equation system

$$\frac{d}{dt}\gamma = R_{XC}^{-1} M_{XC}(\gamma) \left[ T(h(\gamma)) - \gamma \right] \tag{89a}$$

$$\frac{d}{dt} R_{XC} = M_{XC}(\gamma) - R_{XC}. \tag{89b}$$

In (89a) and (89b), $M_X(\gamma) = E X_{Ct} X'_{Ct}$ is computed from the stationary distribution of (48) at a fixed value of $\gamma$. A fixed point of the ODE (89) evidently satisfies

$$\begin{aligned} R_{XC} &= M_{XC}(\gamma) \\ \gamma &= T(h(\gamma)). \end{aligned} \tag{90}$$

Here $R_{XC}$ is the unconditional covariance matrix for $X_C$ computed at the associated value of $\gamma$ satisfying the last two equations of (90). Because $\gamma = T(h(\gamma))$, a fixed point of the ODE is a self-confirming equilibrium.

*Stochastic approximation*

Under the assumption that the gain sequence $\{g_t\}$ eventually behaves like $t^{-1}$, the following points are true:

(a) If the beliefs $\{\gamma_t, R_t\}$ converge, they converge to a rest point of (89).

(b) If a fixed point of the ODE is locally unstable, then the beliefs $\{\gamma_t, R_t\}$ cannot converge to that fixed point.

(c) If the ODE is globally stable about a fixed point, then modified versions of the laws of motion for beliefs exist that make them converge almost surely to the fixed point.[12]

---

[11] See Marcet and Sargent (1989a, 1989b) and Ljung (1977) for the steps.
[12] To obtain global convergence, the algorithms must include a projection facility that interrupts the basic algorithm whenever the $(\gamma, R_{XC})$ threaten to move

(d) This item requires some prior bookkeeping. The state of the system (89) is the list $(\gamma, R_{XC})$ measuring beliefs. Let $\text{col}(R_{XC})$ denote the vector formed by stacking successive columns of the matrix $R_{XC}$. Then by stacking columns of matrices on both sides of (89) we obtain the representation

$$\frac{d}{dt}\begin{bmatrix} \gamma \\ \text{col}(R_{XC}) \end{bmatrix} = g(\gamma, R_{XC}).$$

Define the Jacobian

$$\mathcal{H}(\gamma, R_{XC}) = \frac{d}{d(\gamma, \text{col}R_{XC})'}g(\gamma, R_{XC}).$$

Local stability of the ODE about a fixed point is governed by the eigenvalues of $\mathcal{H}(\gamma_f, R_f)$, where $(\gamma_f, R_f)$ is a fixed point. If all eigenvalues of $\mathcal{H}(\gamma_f, R_f)$ have negative real parts, then $(\gamma, R_f)$ is a locally stable rest point of (89). Under some technical conditions, including that the gains not be absolutely summable, the eigenvalues of $\mathcal{H}(\gamma_f, R_f)$ govern the rate of convergence of the algorithm to a self-confirming equilibrium. A necessary condition for convergence at the rate $T^{.5}$ is that the eigenvalues of $\mathcal{H}(\gamma_f, R_f)$ be bounded from above in modulus by $-.5$.[13] When the eigenvalue of maximum modulus of $\mathcal{H}(\gamma_f, R_f)$ is between $-.5$ and $0$, convergence to a self-confirming equilibrium occurs, but at a slower rate than $T^{.5}$.

---

outside a domain of attraction of the ODE. See Marcet and Sargent (1989a) and Ljung (1977). Some of the simulations below activate a projection facility. Evans and Honkapohja (1998a) discuss the role of the projection facility and results that can be attained without it. When they dispense with the projection facility they sometimes attain convergence of least squares learning algorithms to rational expectations equilibria with probabilities that are positive but less than unity. They display cases with a globally stable ODE that have convergence with probability one in the absence of a projection facility.

[13] See Marcet and Sargent (1995).

When the gain $g_t$ converges to a constant $\bar{g} > 0$, $(\gamma, R_{XC})$ converges to a stationary stochastic process, and not to a fixed set of beliefs.[14]

The constant gain algorithm arrests the force for convergence to a self-confirming equilibrium. This opens the possibility that the inflation outcome from an adaptive version of the model will produce outcomes different from the Nash outcome. I shall explore this possibility using computer simulations. Before looking at the simulations, I describe an adaptive model under the Keynesian identification.

## Adaptation with Keynesian identification

### Government beliefs and behavior

In the adaptive model where the government fits a Phillips curve in the Keynesian direction, each period the government updates its estimate of $\beta$ in the conjectured Phillips curve (35). The government uses RLS to update $\beta_t$, leading to

$$\beta_t = \beta_{t-1} + g_t R_{XK,t}^{-1} X_{Kt} \left[ y_t - \beta_{t-1}' X_{Kt} \right]$$
$$R_{XK,t} = R_{XK,t-1} + g_t [X_{Kt} X_{Kt}' - R_{XK,t-1}]. \tag{91}$$

Here $\{g_t\}$ again is the gain sequence, set at $\{t^{-1}\}$ by least squares.

After applying the invert-the-Phillips-curve operator $\gamma(\beta)$ to $\beta_t$ to get $\gamma_t$, the model works in the way it does with the classical identification scheme. Based on its beliefs, the government computes a feedback rule $h(\gamma_{t-1})$, where $\gamma_{t-1} = \gamma(\beta_{t-1})$. The government sets $y_t$ according to $y_t = h(\gamma_{t-1}) X_{t-1} + v_{2t}$.

---

[14] See Cho (1997) for a study of learning of reputational equilibria in games where beliefs converge to a stochastic differential equation. Cho restricts the gain and other features of the learning dynamics to make the innovation variance of the stochastic differential equation shrink fast enough to attain convergence in distribution to a particular equilibrium.

*Technical details*

The first equation of (91) can be written

$$\beta_t = \beta_{t-1} + g_t R_{XK,t}^{-1} X_{Kt} X_{Kt}' \left\{ \begin{bmatrix} 0 \\ h \end{bmatrix} - \beta_{t-1} \right\}$$
$$+ g_t R_{XK,t}^{-1} X_{Kt} v_{2t}.$$

Think of forming the regression $v_{2t} = \phi' X_{Kt} + \varepsilon_{\phi,t}$, where $\varepsilon_{\phi,t}$ is orthogonal to $X_{Kt}$. Evidently, for a stationary $X_{Kt}$ process, $\phi$ satisfies $\phi = \left( E X_{Kt} X_{Kt}' \right)^{-1} E X_{Kt} v_{2t}$.

Stochastic approximation shows how the limiting dynamics of the system are described by the associated differential equation system

$$\frac{d}{dt} \beta = R_{XK}^{-1} M_{XK}(\beta) \left( \begin{bmatrix} 0 \\ h \end{bmatrix} + \phi - \beta \right) \qquad (92a)$$

$$\frac{d}{dt} R_{XK} = M_{XK}(\beta) - R_{XK} \qquad (92b)$$

where $M_{XK}$ is the moment matrix calculated from (48) at fixed values of $h(\gamma(\beta))$. A rest point of the ODE is evidently

$$\beta = S(\beta)$$
$$R_{XK} = M_{XK}(\beta),$$

where $S(\beta)$ is as defined in (57). Comparing these equations to those for our self-confirming equilibrium with a Keynesian identification, we see that a rest point is a self-confirming equilibrium.

## Simulations

I have simulated both the Keynesian and the classical adaptive systems, using the Kalman filter to implement recursive least squares by setting $R_{1t} = \left( \frac{g_o}{1-g_o} \right) P_{t-1}$ and $R_{2t}$ to a constant. Appendix A shows how the constant gain satisfies $g_o = 1 - \lambda$

where $\lambda \in (0,1)$ is a discount factor applied to past observations. Appendix A describes the initial value of $P_0$ that starts the government with the prior of someone whose only source of information is $T$ periods of data from within a self-confirming equilibrium; $T$ parameterizes the tightness of the government's prior distribution. I set $R_2$ at the value of $E\varepsilon_{Ct}^2$ associated with the self-confirming equilibrium.

All of the simulations set parameters of the true data generating process at the values used to construct the example at the end of Chapter 7: $\rho_1 = \rho_2 = 0, U^* = 5, \delta = .98, \sigma_1 = \sigma_2 = .3$. I initiate the coefficients at self-confirming equilibrium values and start the covariance matrix $P_0$ at a value for the asymptotic covariance matrix of someone with data from $T$ periods in a self-confirming equilibrium. As our computed-by-hand example showed, because the $\rho_j$'s are zero, at self-confirming equilibria of both Keynesian and classical types, $[\,U_t \quad y_t\,]$ is a serially uncorrelated process. Except for details, this example is the same as Sims's (1988) and is a good laboratory for studying how adaptation can generate serial correlation though there is none in the fundamentals.[15] The value of the discount factor $\delta$ is irrelevant within a self-confirming equilibrium (because the $\rho_j$'s are zero), although it becomes relevant for the behavior of the adaptive systems.

## Classical adaptive simulations

In our simulation of the classical adaptive system, the government's Phillips curve is of the form $U_t = \gamma_{t-1}X_{Ct} + \epsilon_{Ct}$, where $X_{Ct} = [y_t, U_{t-1}, U_{t-2}, y_{t-1}, y_{t-2}, 1]$. Soon our attention will turn to the covariation of the estimated constant and the sum of weights on current and lagged inflation $y$.

Recall that the classical self-confirming equilibrium has serially uncorrelated fluctuations of $(U, y)$ around means of $(5,5)$,

---

[15] The example is not identical to Sims's (1988) because he made the government fit a static Phillips curve. Therefore, my discussion of the activation of the induction hypothesis does not apply to Sims's work. Chung (1990) has the government fit a distributed lag Phillips curve.

and that the Keynesian self-confirming equilibrium has fluctuations around means of $(5, 10)$. Figures 8.1 and 8.2 report simulations of the classical system under two specifications, least squares and constant gain. Thus, in Figure 8.1, we set $\lambda = 1, T = 800$; in Figure 8.2, we set $\lambda = .975, T = 300$.

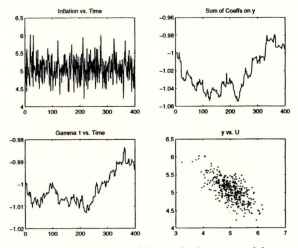

**Figure 8.1.** Simulation of classical adaptive model under decreasing gain (least squares).

The $\{t^{-1}\}$-gain Figure 8.1 resembles a simulation of a self confirming equilibrium. But the long (1,000 periods) Figure 8.2 simulation under constant gain displays aspects of behavior reported by Sims and Chung. The inflation panel shows that inflation starts near the self-confirming equilibrium value, but then drops almost to zero and stays there for a long time. Over time, inflation slowly heads back toward the self-confirming value of 5, only to be propelled back toward zero again. The mean dynamics that pull the system toward the self-confirming equilibrium are opposed by a recurrent force that sends the inflation rate close to the Ramsey outcome (zero inflation). Inspection of the simulated $v_t$ series, which I do not report, revealed that no large shocks prompt the large initial stabilizations or the subsequent smaller ones.

Evidence that the mean dynamics operate slowly is supplied by the eigenvalues of the Jacobian $\mathcal{H}$ described above. For the model under the classical identification with these parameter values, there is a repeated eigenvalue of $-.5$ of multiplicity 6, as well as a repeated eigenvalue of $-1$ associated with the dynamics of the components of $R_{XC}$. Note that one repeated eigenvalue occurs at the boundary of the region within which convergence occurs at a rate corresponding to the square root of the sample size.

Other panels of Figure 8.2a and 8.2b assemble clues about features of the government's beliefs that prompt it to reduce inflation along the simulated sample path. The second and third panels of Figure 8.2a show time series of the sum of coefficients and the constant, respectively, in the estimated Phillips curve. How these two move together is the key to the behavior of inflation. During the first dramatic stabilization episode, the sum of coefficients on current and lagged $y$, shown in panel 2 of Figure 8.2a, jumps from its self-confirming value of $-1$ to nearly zero. Simultaneously, the constant in the estimated Phillips curve drops. These co-movements affect the solution of the Phelps problem, and cause the constant in the decision rule for inflation to behave as in the fourth panel. The constant in the decision rule $h$, shown in the fourth panel of Figure 8.2a, essentially determines the behavior of inflation. As we saw in Chapter 5, a value near zero of the sum of coefficients on inflation activates the induction hypothesis and makes the Phelps problem advise the government to reduce inflation. Values of the sum of coefficients near zero seem to occupy a dominating position along an escape route for most likely deviations away from a self-confirming equilibrium.

Figures 8.2b, 8.2c, and 8.2d add more information about the dynamics of the escape route from the self-confirming equilibrium. [16]

Figure 8.2b plots the sum of coefficients again, and below it the standard error of that sum from the time $t$ covariance matrix of coefficients (denoted $P_{t-1}$ in the Kalman filter formulation of Appendix A). It also plots the slope of the contemporaneous Phillips curve and its standard error. The behavior of the standard errors shows us why the system takes this particular route away from the self-confirming equilibrium. Within the self-confirming equilibrium, the standard error of the sum of weights is about .13. As the initial 80 observations accumulate, the system stays close to the self-confirming equilibrium, but the standard error of the sum of weights approximately doubles. Simultaneously, the standard error on the constant increases (shown in the third panel of Figure 8.2a). Now look at Figures 8.2c and 8.2d, which show 95% and 99% confidence ellipsoids around the sum of the coefficients on current and lagged inflation $y$ (the ordinate) and the constant (the coordinate) in the estimated Phillips curve at various dates $t$. The vertical line at ordinate zero indicates where the induction hypothesis is satisfied. Figure 8.2d plots the confidence ellipsoids for dates surrounding the first stabilization. When near the self-confirming equilibrium early in the simulation, the confidence ellipsoid reveals a trade-off reflected in a negative correlation between the constant and the sum of the weights. Note how the ellipsoid is tilted along an axis that connects the self-confirming equilibrium value $(0, 10)$ with the value of the sum of weights of zero that would activate the induction hypothesis. Figure 8.2c

---

[16]  As mentioned above, a deterministic intertemporal cost minimization problem determines a path around which the stochastic process for beliefs puts most probability. The state of beliefs is a large dimensional object, including the coefficient vector and the covariance matrix of that coefficient vector. The confidence ellipses in the text summarize the escape route from the simulations to highlight the action of the induction hypothesis. The moving confidence ellipsoids in Figure 8.2 and 8.3 are projections of the confidence ellipsoids of $(\gamma, R_{XC})$ and $(\beta, R_{XK})$, respectively, onto smaller spaces.

shows how the confidence ellipsoid grows as observations up to about period 80 accrue, while remaining centered at the self-confirming values. The growing confidence ellipsoids makes the government's econometricians more open to interpreting the data as consistent with Solow and Tobin's distributed lag version of the natural-rate hypothesis.[17] By chance, this happens in the eighties, as Figure 8.2d shows when the Phelps problem directs the government to stabilize.

Figures 8.2c and 8.2d show how after the stabilization occurs, the government's behavior generates a string of serially correlated observations that affirm the induction hypothesis. Notice how the confidence ellipsoids center around the induction hypothesis and how they shrink. Evidently, the stabilization generates observations that temporarily add credibility to the induction hypothesis that prompted it. Our earlier analysis shows that this situation is not self-confirming in the technical sense but is nevertheless reinforcing.

[17] The growing confidence ellipsoids make it as likely that the data drive the estimated Phillips curve away from the induction hypothesis as towards it. The behavior induced by the Phelps problem prevents persistent movements in a direction pointing away from the induction hypothesis.

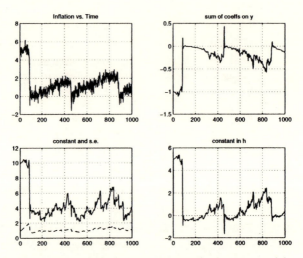

**Figure 8.2a.** Simulation of classical adaptive model under constant gain, $\delta = .98, \lambda = .975$.

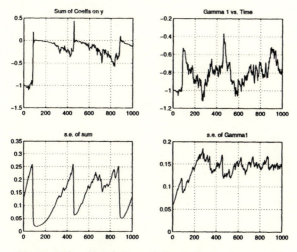

**Figure 8.2b.** Simulation of classical adaptive model under constant gain, $\delta = .98$, $\lambda = .975$.

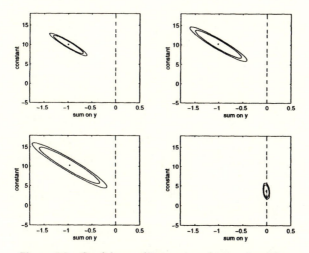

**Figure 8.2c.** Confidence ellipses around sum of weights on $y$ and constant in Phillips curve, evaluated at observation numbers 5, 40, 80, and 100, for classical adaptive model.

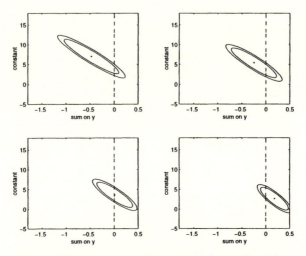

**Figure 8.2d.** Confidence ellipses around sum of weights on $y$ and constant in Phillips curve, evaluated at observation numbers 84, 85, 86, 87, for classical adaptive model.

## *Relation to equilibria under forecast misspecification*

The simulation of the adaptive system exhibits a feature reminiscent of the Chapter 6 and 7 equilibria with optimal misspecified forecasts. There, an incorrect forecasting model without a constant but with a unit root in the inflation forecasting equation, could closely approximate a true model that includes a constant. The sense of approximation there was subtle, because of how both the true and approximating models influenced one another.[18] An approximation mechanism with a similar flavor operates during periods in our simulations that have near-Ramsey outcomes. The approximation is not to a fixed model for the inflation process, but to one that changes as the government's beliefs influence the actual inflation process through the Phelps problem.

---

[18] Recall how the adaptive expectations parameter $C$ disappeared from the list of free parameters.

*Simulation with Keynesian adaptation*

In simulations of the adaptive Keynesian system, the government's estimated Phillips curve is $y_t = \beta_{t-1} X_{Kt} + \epsilon_{Kt}$, where $X_{Kt} = [U_t, U_{t-1}, U_{t-2}, y_{t-1}, y_{t-2}, 1]$. As in our study of the system under the classical identification scheme, I focus on the co-variation of the estimate of the constant and the sum of weights on lagged inflation.

Figures 8.3a–8.3d display a simulation of the adaptive system under the Keynesian identification. This simulation sets $\lambda = .99, T = 300$. The inflation rate starts with a long spell near the self-confirming value of 10, then after a period of turbulence drops to near the Ramsey level and stays there for a long time. There is eventually a burst of inflation back toward a neighborhood of the self-confirming value, but this episode is again followed by a long spell near the Ramsey outcome. The remaining panels of Figures 8.3a and 8.3b again allow us to interpret the stabilization in terms of the eventual activation of the induction hypothesis, together with movements in the estimated slope $\gamma_1$ of the short-run Phillips curve. The system evidently spends much time away from the self-confirming equilibrium, and, like the classical system, recurrently escapes to the Ramsey outcome.

For the system under the Keynesian identification scheme, the mean dynamics in the vicinity of the self-confirming equilibrium issue a warning: the Keynesian counterpart to the Jacobian $\mathcal{H}$ contains a repeated eigenvalue of $-.2$.[19] The $-.2$ eigenvalue leads us to expect a very slow rate of convergence to a self-confirming equilibrium under least squares learning. This sustains long episodes near the Ramsey outcome, because it evidently takes much time for the mean dynamics to drive the system away from the Ramsey outcome.

The various panels of Figure 8.3 again shed light on the escape route away from the self-confirming equilibrium. They tell

---

[19] Of multiplicity six. There is a repeated eigenvalue of $-1$ associated with $R_{XK}$.

a story much like that for the classical identification scheme. The early part of the sample has inflation near the self-confirming equilibrium value. But the data from this period foster growing doubt about the location of the Phillips curve and put higher weight in the direction of the induction hypothesis which, with the Keynesian identification, manifests itself when the sum of the weights on lagged inflation equals one. The confidence ellipsoids gradually spread, while remaining centered on the self-confirming equilibrium values. Eventually, by chance some observations arrive that push the government's estimated Phillips curve toward the induction hypothesis. After the Phelps problem induces a stabilization, the confidence ellipsoids quickly move toward and collapse around the induction hypothesis.

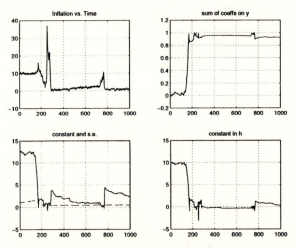

**Figure 8.3a.** Simulation of Keynesian adaptive model under constant gain, $\lambda = .99$.

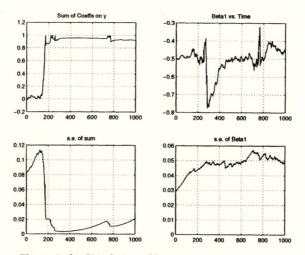

**Figure 8.3b.** Simulation of Keynesian adaptive model under constant gain, $\lambda = .99$.

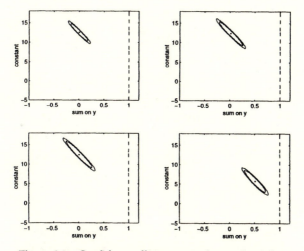

**Figure 8.3c.** Confidence ellipses around sum of weights on $y$ and constant in Phillips curve, evaluated at observation numbers 2, 80, 120, and 160, for Keynesian adaptive model.

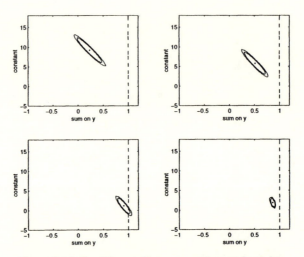

**Figure 8.3d.** Confidence ellipses around sum of weights on $y$ and constant in Phillips curve, evaluated at observation numbers 150, 160, 170, and 200, for Keynesian adaptive model.

*Role of discount factor*

The recurrent stabilizations of inflation toward the Ramsey value of 0 depend on the value of the discount factor $\delta$ being near 1. Other simulations that I have performed, but do not report, show how decreasing $\delta$ causes the value of inflation observed during the recurrent periods of low inflation to rise. This pattern is consistent with the workings of the Phelps problem in conjunction with the induction hypothesis.

## Conclusions

My simulations have features that Sims (1988) and Chung (1990) reported for related systems. For long periods, adaptive governments learn to generate better than Nash or self-confirming outcomes. These results come from the recurrent dynamics induced by adaptation. The mean dynamics that under least squares drive the system toward a self-confirming equilibrium continue to operate under adaptation, but noise lets the adaptive system recurrently escape from a self-confirming equilibrium.[20] Starting from a self-confirming equilibrium, an adaptive algorithm gradually makes the government put enough weight on the induction hypothesis that chance observations eventually promote better than Nash outcomes.

Adaptation makes the government's beliefs a hidden state imparting serial correlation into $[\,U_t \quad y_t\,]$. An outside forecaster would do well to use a random coefficients model, or to make the constant adjustments noted by Lucas (1976).

Our adaptive models thus contain underpinnings for vindicating econometric policy evaluation. It is time to leave the laboratory and turn to history. In the next chapter I take the historical data as inputs and use them to generate parameter estimates and residuals. How the model matches the data, and how it misses, will vindicate or indict econometric policy evaluation.

## Appendix A: RLS and the Kalman filter

### The Kalman filter

Recall the basic Kalman filter from Ljung and Söderström (1983) or Ljung (1992).[21] The Kalman filter is a recursive algorithm for computing least squares estimators of a sequence of hidden state vectors described by a linear stochastic difference equation. The statistical model governing the hidden state $\xi_t$

---

[20] The mechanism of escape is similar to the switches between neighborhoods of rational expectations equilibria that occur in Evans and Honkapohja (1993), except here the escape from an equilibrium is not to another equilibrium.

[21] See Ljung, Pflug, and Walk (1992).

and the observations $z_t, \phi_t$ follows. Let $\xi$ be a vector of coefficients and $\varphi$ a vector of regressors. The model is

$$\xi_t = \xi_{t-1} + w_t, \quad E w_t w_t' = R_{1t} \tag{93a}$$

$$z_t = \xi_t' \varphi_t + e_t, \quad E e_t e_t' = R_{2t}. \tag{93b}$$

Here $\xi_t, \varphi_t$ are each $(n \times 1)$. The aim is to compute $\hat{\xi}_t \equiv E\xi_t | J_t$, where $J_t$ is the time $t$ information set consisting of $z_s, \phi_s, s = 0, \ldots, t$, and $E(\cdot)$ is the least squares projection operator. In our applications, in the classical case, $z_t$ is $U_t$, $\varphi_t$ is $X_{Ct}$, and $\xi_t$ is $\gamma_t$; in the Keynesian case, $z_t$ is $y_t$, $\varphi_t$ is $X_{Kt}$, and $\xi_t$ is $\beta_t$.[22]

The Kalman filter takes the form of the following recursions for $\hat{\xi}_t, P_t$:

$$\hat{\xi}_t = \hat{\xi}_{t-1} + L_t \left[ z_t - \varphi_t' \hat{\xi}_{t-1} \right] \tag{94a}$$

$$L_t = \frac{P_{t-1} \varphi_t}{R_{2t} + \varphi_t' P_{t-1} \varphi_t} \tag{94b}$$

$$P_t = P_{t-1} - \frac{P_{t-1} \varphi_t \varphi_t' P_{t-1}}{R_{2t} + \varphi_t' P_{t-1} \varphi_t} + R_{1t}, \tag{94c}$$

where $P_t = E(\xi_t - \hat{\xi}_t)(\xi_t - \hat{\xi}_t)'$. The recursions are initialized from $P_0, \hat{\xi}_0$.

Consider the case of homoskedastic measurement noise with $R_{2t} = R_2$. It is useful to note that the structure of (94) implies that all that matters in terms of the initial condition is the ratio $\frac{P_0}{R_2}$, so that with an appropriate choice of $P_0$, $R_2$ normalizes.

*Recursive least squares*

In special cases, the Kalman filter leads to a stochastic approximation algorithm called recursive least squares (RLS). Letting the prediction error at the true parameter at time $t$ be $\epsilon(t, \xi) = z_t - \phi_t' \xi$, RLS minimizes a loss function

$$V_T(\xi) = \sum_{t=1}^{T} \kappa_{T,t} \ell(\epsilon(t, \xi), t)$$

---

[22] Thus in the respective cases $\hat{\gamma}_t = E_t \, \gamma_t$ or $\hat{\beta}_t = E_t \, \beta_t$. Note that $\hat{\gamma}_t$ or $\hat{\beta}_t$ is conditioned on time $t$ information.

where $\epsilon(t, \xi) \equiv z_t - \phi_t \xi$ and $\kappa_{T,t}$ discounts past observations geometrically according to

$$\kappa_{T,t} = \lambda^{T-t}, \quad 0 < \lambda \leq 1$$

and where the one-period loss function is $\ell_t = \alpha_t(z_t - \phi_t'\hat{\xi}_{t-1})^2$. The RLS algorithm is

$$\hat{\xi}_t = \hat{\xi}_{t-1} + \alpha_t g_t R_t^{-1}\phi_t \left(z_t - \phi_t'\hat{\xi}_{t-1}\right)$$

$$R_t = R_{t-1} + g_t \left(\alpha_t \phi_t \phi_t' - R_{t-1}\right),$$

where the gain $g_t$ is defined as

$$g_t = \left[\sum_{s=1}^{t} \kappa_{t,s}\right]^{-1}.$$

A constant forgetting factor $\lambda < 1$, leads to $g_t = \left(\frac{1-\lambda^t}{1-\lambda}\right) \rightarrow$ $(1-\lambda)$ as $t \rightarrow +\infty$; $\lambda = 1$ leads to $g_t = \frac{1}{t}$.

## Matching RLS to the Kalman filter

Ljung (1992) pointed out that for a special choice of $R_{1t}, R_{2t}$, the Kalman filter becomes the RLS algorithm. In particular, let

$$R_{1t} = (1/\lambda - 1)P_{t-1} \tag{95a}$$
$$R_{2t} = \lambda/\alpha_t. \tag{95b}$$

For us, the following two cases are interesting. First, when $\lambda = 1$, $R_{1t} = 0$, and $R_{2t} = 1/\alpha_t$. Second, when $\lambda < 1$, $R_{1t}$ is proportional to the last estimate $P_{t-1}$.

We will be considering homoskedastic cases in which $\alpha_t = \alpha$ is constant, which makes the RLS algorithm take the form of the stochastic approximation algorithm

$$\hat{\xi}_t = \hat{\xi}_{t-1} + g_t R_t^{-1}\phi_t(z_t - \phi_t'\hat{\xi}_{t-1})$$

$$R_t = R_{t-1} + g_t \left( \phi_t \phi_t' - R_{t-1} \right).$$

As Ljung (1992) remarked, by leading to a constant gain $g_t$, a forgetting factor operates much like a nonzero $R_{1t}$ coupled with a gain that eventually decreases as $1/t$.

We get an adaptive model by assuming that at time $t$, $\hat{\gamma}_{t-1}$ is used to solve the Phelps problem, which implies

$$y_t = h(\hat{\gamma}_{t-1})X_{t-1} + v_{2t}$$

where $\hat{\gamma}_{t-1}$ is based on information up through $t-1$, namely $U_{t-1}, X_{Ct-1}$, and recall that $X_{t-1}$ includes only information dated $t-1$ and earlier.

### Initial conditions for simulations

For our simulations, we shall set $R_{1t}, R_{2t}$ according to (95) with an initial $P_0$ chosen as follows for the classical case. Associated with a self-confirming equilibrium is a moment matrix $Q = EX_{Ct}X_{Ct}'$, and an associated variance decomposition

$$EU_t^2 = \gamma'Q\gamma + E\varepsilon_{Ct}^2. \tag{96}$$

We set $R_{2t} = \sigma_{Ct}^2 \equiv E\varepsilon_{Ct}^2$, and choose $P_0 = \frac{\sigma_{Ct}^2}{T}Q^{-1}$, where $T$ is a positive integer.[23] This sets $P_0$ equal to the value of the covariance matrix that would be estimated for $\gamma$ by a government that had observed a data record of length $T$ from a self-confirming equilibrium. This procedure gives us a simple one-parameter specification of the government's initial uncertainty about $\gamma$.

For the Keynesian model, we set $Q = EX_{Kt}X_{Kt}'$ from a self-confirming equilibrium, and chose $R_{2t}$ according to the variance decomposition like (96) for the Keynesian direction of fit.

---

[23] Note how with this setting for $P_0$, the choice of $\sigma_{Ct}^2$ has no influence on the behavior of the Kalman filter (94), and amounts just to a normalization.

## *Appendix B: Anticipated utility*

David Kreps (1998) calls our adaptive models of the 1990's anticipated utility models. These models induce transient dynamics by assuming that decision makers adapt a temporarily misspecified model to incorporate the most recent observations and reoptimize along the way. This is a small modification of a rational expectations.

### *Boiler plate recursive rational expectations model*

Assume the following rational expectations model as a base. A representative agent solves the problem whose Bellman equation is

$$v(k, K) = \max_{u}\{R(k, K, u) + \beta E v(k', K')\} \qquad (97)$$

subject to the transition laws

$$k' = g(k, u, \epsilon') \qquad (98)$$
$$K' = G(K, \epsilon'), \qquad (99)$$

where $R(k, K, u)$ is the one period return function and $u$ is the agent's control vector, and $\beta \in (0, 1)$. Variables without primes denote this period values and those with primes denote next period values; $\epsilon$ is a random vector drawn from the c.d.f. $\text{Prob}(\epsilon \leq \bar{\epsilon}) = F(\bar{\epsilon})$.

Here $k$ is the state vector of the representative agent, and $K$ is the average state vector over all agents. The solution of the problem is a timeless policy function

$$u = p(k, K; G). \qquad (100)$$

Substituting (100) into the law of motion (99), and setting $k = K$ gives

$$K' = g(K, p(K, K; G), \epsilon') \equiv T(G)(K, \epsilon'). \qquad (101)$$

This constructs a mapping $T(G)$ from the perceived law of motion $G$ for $K$ to the actual law of motion $T(G)$ for $K$. A rational expectations equilibrium is a fixed point of this mapping.

Notice that calendar time makes no explicit appearance in this description. The laws that link next period values (with primes) to present ones are timeless. An anticipated utility model makes calendar time appear in those laws by withdrawing knowledge of $G$.

*Anticipated utility model*

In Kreps's (1998) sense, an anticipated utility model for this setting could be obtained as follows. In place of (99), the representative agent believes

$$K' = G_t(K, \epsilon'), \tag{102}$$

where for the first time in this appendix, calendar time $t$ appears. The perceived law of motion $G_t$ is formed by an adaptive scheme feeding back on the history of outcomes:

$$G_t = f(G_{t-1}, K_{t-1}). \tag{103}$$

The actual law of motion for the system at $t$ would be

$$K_{t+1} = T(G_t)(K_t, \epsilon_{t+1}), \tag{104}$$

where $T(G)$ is the same operator $T$ defined implicitly via (101), namely, the one derived assuming that $G$ was time-invariant.

We make several observations:

(1) Looked at one way, the recursive structure makes the original rational expectations equilibrium static. The same Bellman equation describes the agent's optimum problem at all dates. These dynamics are a special case of statics.

(2) Kreps's term anticipated utility applies because the setup injects dynamics only by making the representative agent's continuation value time-dated by becoming $E_t v_t(k', K')$, where $E_t$ denotes the expectation, conditional on $k, K$, taken with

respect to the probability distribution induced by the time $t$ model $G_t$.

(3) Because it retains the same functional $p(K, k; G)$ mapping the belief $G$ into the agent's policy, the anticipated utility model is misspecified, at least temporarily (but see point (4)). The misspecification comes from the fact that the functional $p(K, k; G)$ was derived on the assumption of a time-invariant $G$.

(4) The model is arranged so that, depending on details of the recursive learning scheme (103), the misspecification vanishes as $t \to \infty$, because $G_t \to G = T(G)$.

(5) Compared to Bayesian or robust decision makers, these agents ignore their period-by-period model misspecification. A robust decision maker would exercise caution in the face of misspecifications by using a worst case analysis. A Bayesian decision maker would know more about the environment.[24]

---

[24] See Bray and Kreps (1986).

# 9
# Econometric Policy Evaluation

## Introduction

This chapter follows, extends, and revises Chung's (1990) work by estimating adaptive versions of our model under both classical and Keynesian identification schemes. We assume that the shock process $v_t$ is Gaussian. We maximize a Gaussian likelihood function to estimate the free parameters $(\theta, U^*, \rho_1, \rho_2, V_v)$ of the model. Notice that, as in a rational expectations model, this list includes no free parameters describing beliefs. Our primary purpose is to use our econometric results to assess whether and how they might vindicate our model government's econometric policy evaluation procedures.

## Likelihood function

To simulate the adaptive Keynesian model of the preceding chapter, we started with initial conditions for $(y, U, v)$ and for $\beta, R_{XK}$; drew a pseudo-random sequence $\{v_t\}_{t=0}^{T}$; then recursively computed an artificial history $\{y_t, U_t\}_{t=0}^{T}$ and $\{\beta_t, R_{XK,t}\}$, and an associated history for the government's beliefs. The way to estimate the model is to reverse this procedure by starting with the data record $\{y_t, U_t\}_{t=0}^{T}$ together with initial conditions for the government's beliefs and for $(U, y, v)$, and then to use them to solve for a history of residuals $\{v_t\}_{t=0}^{T}$ associated with a particular set of parameter values. A maximum likelihood estimator of the parameters minimizes a particular measure of the size of these residuals.

By expressing the Phillips curve and the formula for $y_t$ as a function of $h(\gamma_{t-1})X_{t-1}$ in reverse forms, we obtain the first two equations of the following five equations that form our adaptive model under the Keynesian identification scheme:

$$v_{1t} - \theta v_{2t} = U_t - (\rho_1 + \rho_2)U_{t-1} + \rho_1\rho_2 U_{t-2} \tag{105a}$$
$$+ \rho_2 v_{1t-1} - \rho_1\theta v_{2t-1} - U^*(1 - \rho_1)(1 - \rho_2)$$
$$v_{2t} = y_t - h(\gamma_{t-1})\, X_{t-1} \tag{105b}$$
$$\gamma_{t-1} = \gamma(\beta_{t-1}) \tag{105c}$$
$$\beta_t = \beta_{t-1} + g_t R_{XK,t}^{-1} X_{Kt} \left[ y_t - \beta_{t-1}' X_{Kt} \right] \tag{105d}$$
$$R_{XK,t} = R_{XK,t-1} + g_t[X_{Kt}X_{Kt}' - R_{XK,t-1}], \tag{105e}$$

where $Ev_t v_t' = \begin{bmatrix} \sigma_1^2 & \sigma_{12} \\ \sigma_{12} & \sigma_2^2 \end{bmatrix} \equiv V_v$, and where we require initial conditions for $[v_{-1}, R_{XK,-1}, \beta_{-1}, U_{-1}, \ldots, U_{-my}, y_{-1}, \ldots, y_{-my}]$. Here (105a), (105b) are versions of the actual Phillips curve (48) and the definition of $v_{2t}$; (105c) applies the invert the Phillips curve operator to deduce $\gamma_{t-1}$ from $\beta_{t-1}$; and (105d)–(105e) repeat (91), the recursive formulas describing the government's learning scheme. Given the initial conditions and a data record for $\{U_s, y_s\}_{s=0}^{T}$, system (105) induces $\{v_t\}_{t=0}^{T}$ and an associated set of government beliefs $\{\beta_t, R_{XK,t}\}_{t=0}^{T}$. The appendix to this chapter displays the Gaussian likelihood function, whose dependence on the data and on the parameters is entirely mediated through their influence on the $v_t$'s via (105).

For the classical version of the model, the likelihood function is defined in a similar way, except that (105c) is dropped, and (105d)–(105e) are replaced by the recursive algorithm (85).

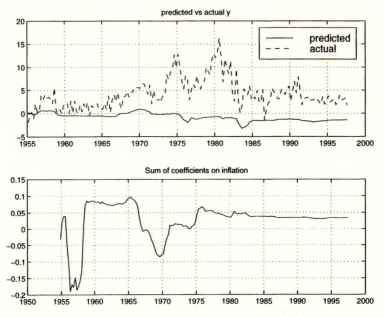

**Figure 9.1.** Actual inflation and outcome recommended by maximum likelihood estimates of classical model.

## *Estimates*

I used the same measures of inflation and unemployment described in Chapter 1. For a sample period 1995I - 1997I, maximum likelihood estimates of the parameters are listed in Tables 3 and 4. I fixed $\delta = .999$ and $\lambda = .985$ to obtain these values.

**Table 3**
Parameter estimates under classical identification

| Parameter | Estimate |
|---|---|
| $\theta$ | .1192 |
| $\rho_1$ | .9145 |
| $\rho_2$ | .5754 |
| $U^*$ | 1.6483 |
| $\log L$ | $-560$ |

**Table 4**
Parameter estimates under Keynesian identification

| Parameter | Estimate |
|-----------|----------|
| $\theta$ | .163 |
| $\rho_1$ | .932 |
| $\rho_2$ | .667 |
| $U^*$ | 2.745 |
| $\log L$ | $-333$ |

For the classical and Keynesian adaptive models, respectively, Figures 9.1 and 9.2a display the one-step ahead prediction for inflation, $\hat{y}_t$, from the best-fitting models.[1] Recall that the prediction $\hat{y}_t$ is the government's target $y$ coming from the Phelps problem, solved at this period's estimate for $\gamma$. The top panels of Figure 9.1 and Figure 9.2a reveal that both versions of the model fit the inflation process badly. The fit is appreciably worse for the model under the classical identification scheme (Figure 9.1). The Keynesian identification scheme leads to a more promising reflection of the inflation pattern, though the gap between predicted and actual, which equals $v_{2t}$, is large after 1973 until 1990. The Keynesian model to some extent matches the acceleration of inflation in the 1970's but underestimates inflation for the next 15 years. The classical model fails even to match the acceleration in inflation leading up to 1970. Its better match to data caused adoption of the Keynesian identification scheme in the U.S. Phillips curve literature. The lower panel of Figure 9.2a shows how the induction hypothesis describes the government's beliefs after the mid 1970's.

Figure 9.2b displays 95% and 99% confidence ellipsoids for the sum of weights on lagged inflation and the constant for $t = 1960, 1965, 1970, 1975, 1980, 1985$. Qualitatively, they resemble the pattern found in our simulations: initially they are away

---

[1] These sample paths are simulations of the models at the maximum likelihood parameter values driven by sample paths of the shocks computed from the appropriate version of (105).

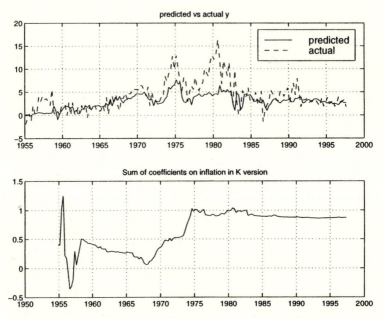

**Figure 9.2a.** Actual inflation and outcome recommended by maximum likelihood estimates of Keynesian model.

from the induction hypothesis, but leave room for doubt. During the 1970's, the point estimates moved, causing the centers of the ellipsoids to shift and doubt to dwindle.

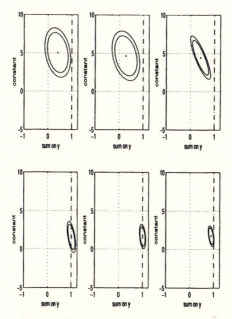

**Figure 9.2b.** 95% and 99% confidence ellipsoids for sum of coefficients on $y$ (ordinate) and constant (coordinate) for first quarter of 1960, 1965, 1970, 1975, 1980, and 1985.

## Interpretation

The large errors from our adaptive models are disappointing if we measure success by a good period-by-period fit. There is a long string of misses in the form of under predictions of inflation during the 1970's, even for the Keynesian model.

But such misses do not necessarily fail to vindicate econometric policy evaluation. To the contrary, the pattern of misses from the estimated models favors vindication.[2] Remembering that

---

[2] This section expresses opinions that I arrived at before receiving a message from Christopher A. Sims interpreting Chung's results in the same way.

the fitted value from the adaptive model is the government's recommendation as time passes extracts vindication from the econometric shortcomings. The fitted values under the Keynesian identification scheme form a sequence of recommendations that confirm the vindication story recounted above. The econometric estimates tell us that unreconstructed Keynesian Phillips curve fitters would have detected the adverse shift in the empirical Phillips curve and, through the induction hypothesis combined with the Phelps problem, would have recommended lowering the inflation rate. Those quantitative policy evaluators would not have concurred with the loosely argued recommendations current in the late 1970's that long lags in expectations made it too costly to disinflate. Our results say that recommendations under classical identification would have been even more timely.

## *Appendix on likelihood function*

Following Chung (1990), we can compute the Gaussian likelihood function of a sample of $\{U_t, y_t\}$ conditional on the initial conditions for $y, U, v, \beta, R_{XK}$.

Because the determinant of the Jacobian of $y_t, U_t$ with respect to $v_t$ is unity, the Gaussian probability distribution of $y_t, U_t$, conditional on $X_{t-1}$, is:

$$L(U_t, y_t \mid X_{t-1}) = (2\pi)^{-1/2} |V_v|^{-1/2} \exp(-\frac{1}{2} v_t' V_v^{-1} v_t).$$

We can condition the likelihood function for a sample $U = [u_1, \cdots, u_T]$, $Y = [y_1, \cdots, y_T]$ on initial values $v_{10}$, $v_{20}$ that we will typically take as zero. Then the Gaussian log likelihood function is:[3]

$$\log L(U, Y \mid X_{-1})$$

---

[3] As usual, we can accelerate the calculation of the likelihood by concentrating out the variance parameters to obtain the estimators, e.g., $V_v = T^{-1} \sum_{t=1}^{T} v_t v_t'$.

$$= \log \left( \sum_{t=1}^{T} (2\pi)^{-1/2} |V_v|^{-1/2} \exp\left[ -\frac{1}{2}\left( v_t' V_v^{-1} v_t \right) \right] \right)$$

$$= -\frac{T}{2} \log 2\pi - \frac{T}{2} \log \det V_v - \frac{1}{2} \sum_{t=1}^{T} \left( v_t' V_v^{-1} v_t \right).$$

# 10
## Triumph or Vindication?

### Expectations and the Lucas critique

The contest between our two accounts of post 1960 U.S. inflation raises various issues about rational expectations models of macroeconomic policies. I began from two benchmark models: a natural-rate model with adaptive expectations for the public, but an optimal policy for the government via the Phelps problem; and a natural unemployment rate model with rational expectations for the public, but an exogenous and arbitrary government policy. Lucas recommended replacing the first benchmark model with the second. Coming to grips with our two stories about post 1960 inflation has caused us to propose other models that make various compromises between these two benchmarks.

Models of credible government policies impose rationality on both the government and the private sector. After recalling Kydland and Prescott's pessimistic prediction drawn from a one-period version of the rational expectations version of a natural rate model, I reviewed how the repeated economy version of the analysis substitutes agnosticism for pessimism. In the end, it seems that after giving up a promise to offer recommendations, the theory of credible policy yields weak predictions about outcomes. In the context of the natural rate example, this makes me hesitate to declare the triumph of the natural rate theory.

As an alternative, following Sims and Chung, I approached history from the opposite pole, turning back from the Lucas Critique and beginning from the Phelps benchmark model. Starting with Phelps's problem, we assume that the government's model of the private sector's behavior is not arbitrary, but is chosen to fit historical data. Variations in the details of the specification led to: (1) self-confirming equilibria, (2) equilibria with misspecified forecasting functions, and (3) 1990's style adaptive expectations (or anticipated utility) models.

In using these models to interpret the data, we reexamined Lucas's Critique and the foundation of the rational expectations econometrics constructed in its wake. Phrases and slogans from the early years of rational expectations have echoed through our account of theory and history: cross-equation restrictions, free parameters, random coefficients, and regime shifts. It is in terms of these phrases that we should evaluate whether our 1990's style adaptive expectations models are closer to 1950's adaptive expectations models or to the 1970's rational expectations models. For instance, take cross-equation restrictions and free parameters and consider the 1990's adaptive model described in Chapter 8. The likelihood function of the adaptive model in Chapter 9 has no free parameters governing expectations.[1] Furthermore, it embodies cross-equation restrictions that period-by-period have the same structure used in rational expectations models.[2] Via its connection to a self-confirming equilibrium as an attractor for its mean dynamics, our 1990's adaptive model satisfies Kreps's (1998) desideratum that it should converge to rational expectations under tranquil conditions.[3] But following Sims (1988), to match the data, our main interest has been in the recurrent dynamics contributed by adaptation. Suspecting that the Phillips curve is prone to wander, the government uses

---

[1] This leaves open whether we want to count the single gain parameter as an extra free parameter relative to a rational expectations model, or whether it should also be counted as a parameter set at a special value for a rational expectations model.

[2] See Hansen and Sargent (1980) for an account of this structure.

[3] Here it is understood that under tranquil conditions, it would be appropriate to set the gain proportional to $\frac{1}{t}$ eventually.

a constant-gain algorithm, an appropriate choice when coefficients wander. Since the government's beliefs influence inflation through the Phelps problem, the constant-gain estimation choice by the government makes a random coefficient specification worthwhile for both the government and the private sector.

This brings us to regime shifts and nonlinearities. Though their behavioral principles remained fixed, our adaptive models generate simulations that exhibit abrupt stabilizations of inflation. These stabilizations defy the time consistency problem in the form of an inferior self-confirming equilibrium pointed to by the system's mean dynamics. Regime shifts occur, not from a change in the government's econometric or policy-making procedures, but from changes in beliefs created by its econometric procedure. The system's nonlinearities, rather than large shocks, explain its behavior. The mathematics of escape routes in the space of approximating models underlies the stabilization. Belief in the induction hypothesis activates inflation-stabilizing (near Ramsey) behavior on the part of the monetary authority. When the constant-gain econometrics let the government use a unit root to approximate a constant with substantial probability (recall the moving confidence ellipses from Chapters 8 and 9), chance occurrences can activate the induction hypothesis.

This returns us to the origin of the induction hypothesis. The induction hypothesis was incorporated almost without comment by Friedman (1957) and Cagan (1956) in formulating the adaptive expectations hypothesis. It was also the basis of Solow's and Tobin's early tests of the natural-rate hypothesis. Cast as villain in Lucas's Critique, the induction hypothesis emerges as hero in delivering the superior long term outcomes in our simulations and the timely recommendations to stabilize that emerge from our econometric estimates in Chapter 9.

This leads us to how models (coefficient vectors and their covariance matrices) approximate one another along the paths of our simulations. The particular escape routes followed by our simulations reflect the ability of a unit root to approximate a mean and thereby to activate the inducation hypothesis. Wrestling with approximation issues, with multiple models in play, caused Sims (1980) to call bounded rationality a wilderness, separated from the tidy one-model structure of rational expectations.

## *Reservations*

I have compared two histories of postwar U.S. inflation: the triumph of natural-rate theory and the vindication of econometric policy evaluation. Each history has the government learning and using a version of the natural unemployment rate hypothesis, either the correct rational expectations version in the triumph story or the approximating adaptive expectations version in the vindication story. The first history is more popular among modern macroeconomists than the second, which seems to defend discredited methods. I consider the second story partly because the first account has contradictions, loose ends, and elements of adaptation, and partly because I think the vindication story captures features of policy making at the Federal Reserve. The contest between our two histories is not rational expectations versus an alternative, because both selectively apply and withdraw from rational expectations.

Our vindication of econometric policy evaluation is an exercise in positive economics, not normative economics. But because it produces near Ramsey outcomes for long periods, this might tempt us to transform it into a normative analysis recommending its econometric policy evaluation procedures. To dampen that temptation, we should recall the simulations presented in Chapter 8. The econometric policy evaluation methods would have yielded sound advice because the U.S. data activated the induction hypothesis. The simulations make us wonder whether that occurred because the econometric policy evaluation procedures ultimately hit upon a stable feature of the price-unemployment dynamics surfacing in the induction hypothesis or whether the historical outcome was a long but temporary episode of low inflation like ones encountered in the simulations. The simulations contain episodes that resemble Arthur Burns as well as ones that look like Paul Volcker. When estimates nearly affirm the induction hypothesis, the mean dynamics of the model point away from the induction hypothesis and toward regions where the Phelps problem recommends resuscitating inflation. It can take a long time for the mean dynamics to push the system back to the self-confirming equilibrium, but it is bound to happen.

For this reason, my exercise in positive economics is not enough to commend its underlying policy making procedures. Theoretical work after Kydland and Prescott has insisted that anti-inflation policy is about designing and adhering to mechanisms that prevent the monetary authorities from choosing sequentially, and from even thinking about the possibility of lowering unemployment through inflation.[4] That work seeks a secure foundation for assuring low inflation under fiat monetary systems. It rejects the idea that chance will lead policy makers armed with an approximate model eventually to learn to do approximately the right thing.

In the end, though our simulations and econometric evidence bolster the vindication of econometric policy evaluation story, we hope that this is the wrong story. We hope instead that policy makers somehow have learned a correct rational expectations version of the natural rate hypothesis and have found devices to commit themselves to low inflation. Otherwise, the mean dynamics governing adaptation threaten eventually to rekindle inflation.

---

[4]  See Rogoff (1985).

# Glossary

ADAPTIVE EXPECTATIONS (1950's): A model making people's expectations of a variable a geometric weighted average of past values of that variable.

ADAPTIVE EXPECTATIONS (1990's): Application of a recursive statistical method for updating estimates of an empirical relationship.

CREDIBILITY PROBLEM: The finding that a Ramsey outcome is better than the Nash outcome – it has higher inflation but the same unemployment.

DRIFTING COEFFICIENTS MODEL: An econometric relationship among variables with parameters evolving randomly.

EMPIRICAL PHILLIPS CURVE: A statistical relationship between distributed lags of inflation and unemployment.

ESCAPE ROUTE: An adaptive system's most likely path of escape from a self-confirming equilibrium.

EXPECTATIONAL PHILLIPS CURVE: A Phillips curve that shifts when people's expectations of inflation shift.

GOVERNMENT BEST RESPONSE: The government's best choice of inflation, given people's expectations of inflation.

INDUCTION HYPOTHESIS: A restriction on people's expectations. It states that if a variable remains constant long enough, people's expectations of that variable will equal that constant.

KEYNESIAN AND CLASSICAL DIRECTIONS: Alternative econometric conditions (orthogonalizations of innovations) used to estimate an empirical Phillips curve.

MEAN DYNAMICS: An ordinary differential equation describing the convergence of an adaptive system to a self-confirming equilbrium.

NASH EQUILIBRIUM: A situation where (1) people's expectations are rational, and (2) inflation is a government best response to people's expectations.

NASH OUTCOME: The inflation and unemployment rates in a Nash equilibrium.

NATURAL UNEMPLOYMENT RATE: The unemployment rate when people's expectations about inflation are realized.

PHELPS PROBLEM: Given an empirical Phillips curve, a government optimization problem for choosing paths of inflation and unemployment.

PHILLIPS CURVE: An inverse relationship between inflation and unemployment.

RAMSEY PROBLEM: The government seeks the rational expectations equilbrium with the best unemployment, inflation pair.

RAMSEY OUTCOME: Solution of the Ramsey problem.

RATIONAL EXPECTATIONS EQUILIBRIA: Outcomes that on average equal peoples' expectations about them.

SELF-CONFIRMING EQUILIBRIUM: An empirical Phillips curve and outcomes for inflation and unemployment that emerge when (1) the government chooses inflation to solve the Phelps problem; (2) people's expectations are rational; and (3) an expectational Phillips curve actually governs the inflation-unemployment rate relationship.

# References

Abreu, Dilip (1988), 'On the Theory of Infinitely Repeated Games with Discounting'. *Econometrica*, March, Vol. 56, No. 2, pp. 383–396.

_____ David Pearce, and Ennio Stacchetti (1986), 'Optimal Cartel Equilibria with Imperfect Monitoring'. *Journal of Economic Theory*, June, Vol. 39, No. 1, pp. 251–269.

_____ _____ _____ (1990), 'Toward a Theory of Discounted Repeated Games with Imperfect Monitoring'. *Econometrica*, September, Vol. 58, No. 5, pp. 1041–1063.

Anderson, Evan, Lars P. Hansen, Ellen McGrattan, and Thomas Sargent (1996), 'Mechanics of Forming and Estimating Dynamic Linear Economies'. In Hans Amman, David Kendrick, and John Rust (eds.), *Handbook of Computational Economics, Vol. 1*. Amsterdam, North Holland Publishing Co..

Atkeson, Andrew (1991), 'International Lending with Moral Hazard and Risk of Repudiation'. *Econometrica*, July, Vol. 59, No. 4, pp. 1069–1089.

Ball, Laurence (1995), 'Time-consistent policy and persistent changes in inflation'. *Journal of Monetary Economics*, November, Vol. 36, No. 2, pp. 329–350.

Barro, Robert J. and David B. Gordon (1983), 'Rules, Discretion, and Reputation in a Model of Monetary Policy'. *Journal of Monetary Economics*, July, Vol. 12, No. 1, pp. 101–121.

_____ _____ (1983), 'A Positive Theory of Monetary Policy in a Natural Rate Model'. *Journal of Political Economy*, August, Vol. 91, pp. 589–610.

Baxter, Marianne (1985), 'The Role of Expectations in Stabilization Policy'. *Journal of Monetary Economics*, May, Vol. 15, No. 3, pp. 343–362.

_____ and Robert G. King (1995), 'Measuring Business Cycles: Approximate Band-Pass Filters for Economic Time Series'. Mimeo, February, NBER Working Paper No. 5022.

Blackwell, D. and L. Dubins (1962), 'Merging of opinions with increasing information'. *Annals of Mathematical Statistics*, Vol. 33, pp. 882–886.

Blinder, Alan S. (1998), *Central Banking in Theory and Practice*. M.I.T. Press, Cambridge, MA.

Borges, Jorge Luis (1962), *Labyrinths*. New Directions Publishing Company, New York.

Bray, Margaret M. (1982), 'Learning, Estimation, and the Stability of Rational Expectations'. *Journal of Economic Theory*, April, Vol. 26, No. 2, pp. 318–339.

_____ and Nathan E. Savin (1986), 'Rational Expectations Equilibria, Learning, and Model Specification'. *Econometrica*, September, Vol. 54, No. 5, pp. 1129–1160.

_____ and David M. Kreps (1987), 'Rational Learning and Rational Expectations'. In Feiwel, George R. (eds.), *Arrow and the Ascent of Modern Economic Theory*. New York University Press, New York, pp. 597-625.

Brock, William A. and Blake D. LeBaron (1996), 'A Dynamic Structural Model for Stock Return Volatility and Trading Volume'. *Review of Economics and Statistics*, February, Vol. 78, No. 1, pp. 94–110.

_____ and C. Hommes (1997), 'A Rational Route to Randomness'. *Econometrica*, September, Vol. 65, No. 5, pp. 1059–1095.

Bucklew, J. A. (1990), *Large Deviation Techniques in Decision, Simulation and Estimation*. New York, John Wiley.

Cagan, Philip (1956), 'The Monetary Dynamics of Hyperinflation'. In Milton Friedman (eds.), *Studies in the Quantity Theory of Money*. Chicago: University of Chicago Press.

Chang, Roberto (1996), 'Credible Monetary Policy with Long Lived Agents: Recursive Approaches'. Mimeo, November, Federal Reserve Bank of Atlanta, Working Paper series: 96-20.

Chari, V.V. and Patrick J. Kehoe (1990), 'Sustainable Plans'. *Journal of Political Economy*, August, Vol. 98, No. 4, pp. 783–802.

_____ _____ and Edward C. Prescott (1989), 'Time Consistency and Policy'. In Robert Barro (eds.), *Modern Business Cycle Theory*. Harvard University Press, Cambridge, Massachusetts, pp. 265–305.

_____ Lawrence Christiano, and Martin Eichenbaum (1996), 'Expectations, Traps and Discretion'. Mimeo, April, NBER Working Paper: 5541, Cambridge, Mass.

Chen, Xiaohong(1993), 'Asymptotic Properties of Recursive M-estimators in an Infinite-dimensional Hilbert Space'. Ph.D. dissertation, Dept.of Economics, Univ of Calif., San Diego, July.

_____ and Halbert White (1992), 'Asymptotic Properties of Some Projection-based Robbins-Monro Procedures in a Hilbert Space'. Mimeo, Department of Economics, University of California at San Diego, Discussion paper 46, November.

_____ _____ (1998), 'Nonparametric Adaptive Learning with Feedback'. *Journal of Economic Theory*, vol. 81, 1998 (in press).

Cho, In-Koo and Akihiko Matsui (1995), 'Induction and the Ramsey Policy'. *Journal of Economic Dynamics and Control*, July - September, Vol. 19, No. 5-7, pp. 1113–1140.

_____ (1997a), 'Learning to coordinate in repeated coordination games'. Mimeo, Brown University.

_____ (1997b), 'Convergence of Least Squares Learning in Discontinuous Self-Referential Stochastic Models'. Mimeo, Brown University.

Chung, Heetaik (1990), 'Did Policy Makers Really Believe in the Phillips Curve? An Econometric Test'. Ph.D. dissertation, University of Minnesota, November.

Cooley, Thomas F. and Edward C. Prescott (1973), 'An Adaptive Regression Model'. *International Economic Review*, June, Vol. 14, No. 2, pp. 364–371.

De Long, J. Bradford (1997), 'America's Only Peacetime Inflation: The 1970's'. In Christina D. Romer and David Romer (eds.), *Reducing Inflation*. NBER Studies in Business Cycles, Volume 30.

Doan, T., Robert Litterman, and Christopher Sims (1984), 'Forecasting and Conditional Projections Using Realistic Prior Distributions'. *Econometric Reviews*, Vol. 3, No. 1, pp. 1–100.

Dupuis, Paul and Harold J. Kushner (1985), 'Stochastic Approximations Via Large Deviations: Asymptotic Properties'. *Siam J. Control and Optimization,* September, Vol. 23, pp. 675–696.

_____ _____ (1987), 'Asymptotic Behavior of Constrained Stochastic Approximations via the Theory of Large Deviations'. *Probability Theory and Related Fields,* February, Vol. 75, pp. 223–244.

_____ _____ (1989), 'Stochastic Approximation and Large Deviations: Upper Bounds and w.p.1 Convergence'. *Siam J. Control and Optimization,* September, Vol. 27, pp. 1108–1135.

_____ and Richard S. Ellis (1997), *A Weak Convergence Approach to the Theory of Large Deviations.* New York, John Wiley and Sons.

Evans, G. W. and Seppo Honkapohja (1993), 'Adaptive Forecasts, Hysteresis, and Endogenous Fluctuations'. *Economic Review, Federal Reserve Bank of San Francisco,* No. 1, pp. 3–13.

_____ _____(1994), 'Convergence of Least Squares Learning to a non-stationary equilibrium'. *Economic Letters,* October, Vol. 46, No. 2, pp. 131–136.

_____ _____ (1995), 'Local Convergence of Recursive Learning to Steady States and Cycles in Stochastic Nonlinear Models'. *Econometrica,* January, Vol. 63, No. 1, pp. 195-226.

_____ _____(1998a ), 'Economic Dynamics with Learning: New Stability Results'. *Review of Economic Studies,* Vol. 65, No. 1, pp. 23-44.

_____(1998b), 'Learning Dynamics'. In John B. Taylor and Michael Woodford (eds.), *Handbook of Macroeconomics.* Elsevier, Amsterdam, in press.

_____ _____(1998c), 'Adaptive Learning and Macroeconomic Dynamics'. Mimeo, University of Oregon and University of Helsinki.

_____ _____ Ramon Marimon (1997), 'Fiscal Constraints and Monetary Stability'. Mimeo, Firenze, Italy.European University Institute

Fischer, Stanley and Lawrence H. Summers (1989), 'Should Governments Learn to Live with Inflation?'. *American Economic Review, Papers and Proceedings,* Vol. 79, No. 2, pp. 382–387.

_____ (1986), 'Contracts, Credibility, and Disinflation'. In Stanley Fischer (eds.), *Indexing, Inflation, and Economic Policy.* Cambridge, Mass.: M.I.T. Press, pp. 221-245.

Fleming, Wendell H. and Raymond W. Rishel (1975), *Deterministic and Stochastic Optimal Control.* New York, Heidelberg, Berlin.Springer-Verlag

Foster, Dean and H. Peyton Young (1990), 'Stochastic Evolutionary Game Dynamics'. *Theoretical Population Biology,* Vol. 38, pp. 219–232.

Freidlin, M. I. and A.D. Wentzell (1984), *Random perturbations of dynamical systems.* New York : Springer-Verlag.

Friedman, Milton (1957), *A Theory of the Consumption Function.* Princeton, Princeton University Press.

_____ (1968), 'The Role of Monetary Policy'. *American Economic Review,* Vol. 58, No. 1, pp. 1–17.

Fudenberg, Drew and David K. Levine (1993), 'Self-Confirming Equilibrium'. *Econometrica,* May, Vol. 61, No. 3, pp. 523–545.

_____ _____ (1995), 'Consistency and Cautious Fictitious Play'. *Journal of Economic Dynamics and Control,* July - September, Vol. 19, No. 5-7, pp. 1065–1089.

Fuhrer, Jeffrey C. (1995), 'The Phillips Curve is Alive and Well'. *New England Economic Review,* March/April, pp. 41–55.

Gordon, Robert J. (1970), 'The Recent Acceleration of Inflation and its Lessons for the Future'. In Arthur Okun and George Perry (eds.), *Brookings Papers on Economic Activity.* Vol. 0, No. 1, pp. 8–41.

—— (1971), 'Inflation in Recession and Recovery'. *Arthur Okun and George Perry*, Brookings Papers on Economic Activity.Vol. 0, No. 1, pp. 105–166

—— (1977), 'Can the Inflation of the 1970's be Explained?'. *Arthur Okun and George Perry*, Brookings Papers on Economic Activity.Vol. 1 No. 0, pp. 253–277

Granger, C.W.J. (1996), 'The Typical Spectral Shape of an Economic Variable'. *Econometrica*, Vol. 34, No. 1, pp. 150–161.

Green, Edward J. and Robert H. Porter (1984), 'Non-Cooperative Collusion Under Imperfect Price Information'. *Econometrica*, January, Vol. 52, No. 1, pp. 89–100.

Gulinsky, O.V. and A. Yu Veretennikov (1993), *Large Deviations for Discrete Time Processes with Averaging*. VSP, Utrecht, The Netherlands.

Hansen, Lars Peter and Thomas Sargent (1993), 'Seasonality and Approximation Errors in Rational Expectations Models'. *Journal of Econometrics*, January/February, Vol. 55, No. 1-2, pp. 21–55.

Hurwicz, Leonid (1951), 'Comment'. *Conference on Business Cycles*, National Bureau of Economic Research, New York, pp. 416–20.

Ireland, Peter N. (1995), 'Optimal Disinflationary Paths'. *Journal of Economic Dynamics and Control*, November, Vol. 19, No. 8, pp. 1429–1448.

—— (1997a), 'Sustainable Monetary Policies'. *Journal of Economic Dynamics and Control*, November, Vol. 22, No. 1, pp. 87-108.

—— (1997b), 'Stopping Inflations, Big and Small'. *Journal of Money, Credit, and Banking*, November, Vol. 29, No. 4, part 2, pp. 759-775.

—— (1997c), 'Does the Time-Consistency Problem Explain the Behavior of Inflation in the United States?'. Mimeo, New Brunswick, New Jersey.Rutgers University

Kalai, Ehud and E. Lehrer (1993), 'Rational learning leads to Nash equilibrium'. *Econometrica*, September, Vol. 61, No. 5, pp. 1019-1045.

Kandori, Michihiro, George J. Mailath, and Rafael Rob (1993), 'Learning, Mutation, and Long Run Equilibria in Games'. *Econometrica*, January, Vol. 61, No. 1, pp. 29–56.

King, Robert G. and Mark W. Watson (1994), 'The Post-War U.S. Phillips Curve: A Revisionist Econometric History'. *Carnegie-Rochester Conf. Series on Public Policy*, December, Vol. 41, No. 0, pp. 157–219.

—— James H. Stock, and Mark Watson (1995), 'Temporal Instability of the Unemployment-Inflation Relationship'. *Economic Perspectives, Federal Reserve Bank of Chicago*, May/June, Vol. 19, No. 3, pp. 2–12.

Kreps, David (1990), *Game Theory and Economic Modeling*. Oxford University Press, New York.

—— (1998), 'Anticipated Utility and Dynamic Choice'. Mimeo, 1997 Schwartz lecture, Northwestern University, Evanston.

Kurz, Mordecai (1994), 'On the Structure and Diversity of Rational Beliefs'. *Economic Theory*, October, Vol. 46, No. 6, pp. 877–900.

Kushner, Harold J. and Dean S. Clark (1978), *Stochastic Approximation Methods for Constrained and Unconstrained Systems*. Springer-Verlag, New York.

—— and G. George Yin (1997), *Stochastic Approximation Algorithms and Applications*. Springer, New York.

Kydland, Finn and Edward C. Prescott (1977), 'Rules Rather than Discretion: the Inconsistency of Optimal Plans'. *Journal of Political Economy*, June, Vol. 85, No. 3, pp. 473–491.

Leamer, Edward (1978), *Specification Searches: ad hoc inference with nonexperimental data*. New York, Wiley.

Ljung, Lennart (1977), 'Analysis of Recursive Stochastic Algorithms'. *IEEE Transactions on Automatic Control*, Vol. AC-22, pp. 551-575.

Ljung, Lennart and Torsten Söderström (1993), *Theory and Practice of Recursive Identification*. MIT Press, Cambridge, Mass.

Ljungqvist, Lars and Thomas J. Sargent (forthcoming), *Recursive Macroeconomic Theory*. In preparation.

Lucas, Robert E., Jr. (1972), 'Econometric Testing of the Natural Rate Hypothesis'. In The Econometrics of Price Determination: Conference, October 30-31, 1970 (eds.), *Otto Eckstein*. Washington: Board of Governors, Federal Reserve System.

———— (1976), 'Econometric Policy Evaluation: A Critique'. In Karl Brunner and Alan Meltzer (eds.), *The Phillips Curve and Labor Markets*. Carnegie-Rochester Conf. Ser. Public Policy.Vol. 1, pp. 19-46

———— (1979), 'A Review: Paul McCracken et. al., Towards Full Employment and Price Stability, A Report to the OECD by a Group of Independent Experts'. In Karl Brunner and Alan Meltzer (eds.), *Policies for Employment, Prices, and Exchange Rates*. Carnegie-Rochester Series on Public Policy, Vol. 11, pp. 161–158.

———— (1980), 'Two Illustrations of the Quantity Theory of Money'. *American Economic Review*, December, Vol. 70, No. 5, pp. 1005–1014.

———— and Edward C. Prescott (1971), 'Investment Under Uncertainty'. *Econometrica*, September, Vol. 39, No. 5, pp. 659–681.

———— and Thomas J. Sargent (1981), 'After Keynesian Macroeconomics'. In Robert E. Lucas and Thomas J. Sargent (eds.), *Rational Expectations and Econometric Practice*. University of Minnesota Press.Minneapolis, University of Minnesota Press

McCall, John (1970), 'Economics of Information and Job Search'. *Quarterly Journal of Economics*, February, Vol. 84, No. 1, pp. 113–126.

Marcet, Albert and Juan Pablo Nicolini (1997), 'Recurrent Hyperinflations and Learning'. Mimeo, Barcelona, Universitat Pampeu Fabra.

———— and Sargent, Thomas J. (1989), 'Convergence of Least Squares Learning Mechanisms in Self Referential Linear Stochastic Models'. *Journal of Economic Theory*, August, Vol. 48, No. 2, pp. 337–368.

———— ———— (1989b), 'Convergence of Least Squares Learning in Environments with Hidden State Variables and Private Information'. *Journal of Political Economy*, December, Vol. 97, No. 6, pp. 1306–22.

———— ———— (1989c), 'Least Squares Learning and the Dynamics of Hyperinflation'. In William Barnett, John Geweke and Karl Shell (eds.), *Economic Complexity: Chaos, Sunspots, and Nonlinearity*. Cambridge University Press.

———— ———— (1992), 'The Convergence of Vector Autoregressions to Rational Expectations Equilibrium'. In Alessandro Vercelli and Nicola Dimitri (eds.), *Macroeconomics: A Survey of Research Strategies*. Oxford University Press, New York, pp. 139–164.

———— ———— (1993), 'Speed of Convergence of Recursive Least Squares Learning with ARMA Perceptions'. In Alan Kirman and Mark Salmon (eds.), *Learning and Rationality in Economics*. Basil Blackwell, Oxford.

Marimon, Ramon and Ellen R. McGrattan (1993), 'On Adaptive Learning in Strategic Games'. In Alan Kirman and Mark Salmon (eds.), *Learning and Rationality in Economics*. Basil Blackwell, Oxford.

_____ (1997), 'Learning from Learning in Economics'. In David Kreps and Kenneth Wallis (eds.), *Advances in Economics and Econometrics: Theory and Applications. Seventh World Congress, Volume 1*. Cambridge University Press.

Maskin, Eric and Jean Tirole (1994), 'Markov Perfect Equilibrium'. Mimeo, Harvard Institute of Economic Research, Discussion Paper 1698.

Muth, John F. (1960), 'Optimal Properties of Exponentially Weighted Forecasts'. *Journal of the American Statistical Association*, Vol. 55, No. 290, pp. 299–306.

_____ (1961), 'Rational Expectations and the Theory of Price Movements'. *Econometrica*, July, Vol. 29, No. 3, pp. 315–335.

McCracken, Paul, et. al. (1977), *Towards Full Employment and Price Stability: A Report to the OECD by a Group of Independent Experts*. Paris: Organization for Economic Cooperation and Development.

Mustafa, Denis and Keith Glover (1990), *Minimum Entropy $H^\infty$ Control*. Berlin, New York, Springer-Verlag.

Myerson, Roger (1998), 'Large Poisson Games'. *Journal of Economic Theory*, forthcoming.

Nyarko, Yaw (1994), 'Bayesian Learning Leads to Correlated Equilibria in Normal Form Games'. *Economic Theory*, October, Vol. 4, No.6, pp. 821–841.

Parkin, Michael (1993), 'Inflation in North America'. In Kumiharo Shigehara (eds.), *Price Stabilization in the 1990's*. pp. 47–83.

Phelan, Christopher and Ennio Stacchetti (1997), 'Subgame Perfect Equilibrium in a Ramsey Taxes Model'. Mimeo, Northwestern University and University of Michigan.

Phelps, Edmund S. (1967), 'Phillips Curves, Expectations of Inflation and Optimal Unemployment Over Time'. *Economica*, August, Vol. 2, No. 3, pp. 22–44.

Prescott, Edward C. (1967), 'Adaptive Decision Rules for Macro Economic Planning'. Ph.D. dissertation, Graduate School of Industrial Administration, Carnegie Institute of Technology.

Rogoff, Kenneth (1985), 'The Optimal Degree of Commitment to an Intermediate Monetary Target'. *Quarterly Journal of Economics*, November, Vol. 100, No. 4, pp. 1169–1189.

_____ (1989), 'Reputation, Coordination, and Monetary Policy'. In Robert Barro (eds.), *Modern Business Cycle Theory*. Harvard University Press, Cambridge, Massachusetts, pp. 236-264.

Samuelson, Paul A. and Robert M. Solow (1960), 'Analytical Aspects of Anti-Inflation Policy'. *American Economic Review*, May, Vol. 50, No. 2 , pp. 177–194.

Sargent, Thomas J. (1971), 'A Note on the Accelerationist Controversy'. *Journal of Money, Credit, and Banking*, August, Vol. 3, No.3, pp. 721–725.

_____ and Neil Wallace (1976), 'Rational Expectations and the Theory of Economic Policy'. *Journal of Monetary Economics*, April, Vol. 2, No. 2, pp. 169–183.

_____ (1984), 'Autoregressions, Expectations, and Advice'. *American Economic Review, Papers and Proceedings*, May, Vol. 74, No.2, pp. 408–415.

_____ (1986), *Rational Expectations and Inflation*. Harper & Row, New York.

_____ (1993), *Bounded Rationality in Macroeconomics*. Oxford University Press, New York.

_____ and François R. Velde (1995), 'Macroeconomic Features of the French Revolution'. *Journal of Political Economy*, June, Vol. 103, No. 3, pp. 474–518.

Sims, Christopher A. (1971), 'Discrete Approximations to Continuous Time Distributed Lags in Econometrics'. *Econometrica*, May, Vol. 39, No. 3, pp. 545–563.

_____ (1972), 'The Role of Approximate Prior Restrictions on Distributed Lag Estimation'. *Journal of the American Statistical Association*, March, Vol. 67, No. 1, pp. 169–175.

_____ (1980), 'Macroeconomics and Reality'. *Econometrica*, January, Vol. 48, No.1, 1–48.

_____ (1982), 'Policy Analysis with Econometric Models'. *Brookings Papers on Economic Activity*, No. 1, pp. 107–152.

_____ (1988), 'Uncertainty across Models'. *American Economic Review*, May, Vol. 78, No. 2, pp. 163–167.

_____ (1988), 'Projecting Policy Effects with Statistical Models'. *Revista de Analisis Economico*, Vol. 3, pp. 3–20.

_____ (1993), 'Rational Expectations Modeling with Seasonally Adjusted Data'. *Journal of Econometrics*, January/February, Vol. 55, No. 1-2, pp. 9–19.

Solow, Robert M. (1968), 'Recent Controversy on the Theory of Inflation: an Eclectic View'. In Stephen Rousseaus (eds.), *Proceedings of a Symposium on Inflation: Its Causes, Consequences, and Control*. New York, New York University.

Stacchetti, Ennio (1991), 'Notes on Reputational Models in Macroeconomics'. Mimeo, Stanford University, September.

Staiger, Douglas, James H. Stock, and Mark W. Watson (1996), 'How Precise are Estimates of the Natural Rate of Unemployment'. Mimeo, NBER Working Paper 5477.

Stokey, Nancy L. (1989), 'Reputation and Time Consistency'. *American Economic Review, Papers and Proceedings*, May, Vol. 79, No. 2, pp. 134–139.

_____ (1991), 'Credible Public Policy'. *Journal of Economic Dynamics and Control*, October, Vol. 15, No. 4, pp. 627–656.

Taylor, John B. (1975), 'Monetary Policy during a Transition to Rational Expectations'. *Journal of Political Economy*, October, Vol. 83, No. 5, pp. 1009–1021.

_____ (1993), 'Discretion Versus Policy Rules in Practice'. *Carnegie-Rochester Conf. Series on Public Policy*, December, Vol. 39, No. 0, pp. 195–214.

_____ (1997), 'America's Peacetime Inflation: The 1970's'. In Christina D. Romer and David Romer (eds.), *Reducing Inflation*. NBER Studies in Business Cycles, Volume 30, 1997.

Tobin, James (1968), 'Discussion'. In Stephen Rousseaus (eds.), *Proceedings of a Symposium on Inflation: Its Causes, Consequences, and Control*. New York, New York University.

Townsend, Robert (1983), 'Forecasting the Forecasts of Others'. *Journal of Political Economy*, August, Vol. 91, No. 4, pp. 546–588.

White, Halbert (1982), 'Maximum Likelihood Estimation of Misspecified Models'. *Econometrica*, January, Vol. 50, No. 1, pp. 1–25.

_____ (1992), *Maximum Likelihood Estimation of Misspecified Models*. Cambridge and Oxford; Blackwell, pp. 259–288.

Whiteman, Charles H. (1984), 'Lucas on the Quantity Theory: Hypothesis Testing without Theory'. *American Economic Review*, September, Vol. 74, No. 4, pp. 742–749.

Woodford, Michael (1990), 'Learning to Believe in Sunspots'. *Econometrica*, March, Vol. 58, No. 2, pp. 277–307.

# Author Index

# Subject Index